GUSTAVE EIFFEL:
BEYOND THE TOWER
Vol. 1

NORTHWATER

CONSTANTINE ISSIGHOS

Copyright 2013 C Constantine Issighos. Published in Canada. Printed in U.S.A. No part of this book may be reproduced or transmitted in any form or any means, electronic or mechanical, including photocopying, recording, and/or by any information storage and retrieval system except by a reviewer who may quote a brief passages in a review to be printer I a newspaper, magazine, or on the Internet without written permission in writing from the author/publisher. For more information please contact: issighos@gmail.com

NORTHWATER is an imprint of Awaqkuna Books Inc.

THE GUSTAVO EIFFEL EXPLORATION SERIES

GUSTAVO EIFFEL: BEYOND THE TOWER
VOL. I

Library and Archives Canada

ISBN 978-1-927845-00-4

Library and Archives Canada Cataloging in Publication.

Graffic Design: Sergio Gonzales Fansanando, Ica - Perú

ATTENTION: BOOK CLUBS, BOOK STORES, BOOK DISTRIBUTORS, PUBLIC or PRIVATE LIBRARIES, UNIVERSITIES AND COLLEGES: QUANTITY DISCOUNTS ARE AVAILABLE ON BULK PURCHASESOF THIS BOOK SERIES.

ACKNOWLEDGEMENTS

My investigation to confirm the authenticity of various Eiffel works in the Americas has taken approximately five years. In the course of these years, I travelled to nine countries and visited countless places which were recommended by tourist guides, cultural officials, librarians, taxi drivers, Directors of museums, municipal record keepers, to name just a few of the people who tried to help with my investigation. Most informed or misinformed persons that I talked to offered their opinions based on secondary information that they had acquired from others during their lifetime.

In my brief article Reality and Myth, in Gustave Eiffel: Beyond the Tower, Vol. I, I explained the complications that exist with verifying genuine works of Eiffel, against countless cultural speculations, tourist promotions and plain misinformation.

As such, casual conversations with knowledgeable persons and discovering peripheral evidence about Eiffel's particular works were the only avenues I had at my disposal. Such peripheral evidence could be a commemoration plaque attached to the monument itself, a "Made by" mark impressed upon it, a recorded public figure's speech during a public event, a newspaper article about the cultural importance of an iron structure made by Eiffel, or the casual scribbling done by an official in a local or national ministry.

A case in point is the Bolivar Bridge of Arequipa, Peru, where non-official records show that the iron structure of the bridge was manufactured in France. This claim is far from the truth. The Bolivar Bridge may have been designed by Eiffel, but its iron parts were made by the Phoenix Iron Co. of Thailand, France's colony in Indochina at the time. This fact was confirmed by the "Made by" markings on the bridge's central column. It is a well-known historical fact that Eiffel's Company had many joint ventures with foundries in Europe and elsewhere. However, I could not confirm the association between Eiffel's Construction CIE of Paris and Phoenix Iron Co. of Thailand. The latter's extensive metal-forge record, however, was confirmed in an article written in Engineering News, September to December 1879. My personal discovery of this fact was appreciated by local officials who corrected their own records.

I spent many days and countless hours with a large number of officials from Ministries of Culture, Heritage and Monuments, Directors of museums, clergy of Churches and Cathedrals in order to verify records of authenticity for each structure. In the course of doing so, I encountered ignorance, trickery, corruption and also genuine offers of support. At times, I over-extended the good people's "welcome."

I want to express my sincere gratitude to all of the people who have helped me in my sometimes overwhelming task, whether they were from Peru, Brazil, Argentina, Chile, Ecuador, Bolivia or Mexico. Special gratitude goes to the Directors of municipal museums for their professionalism and genuine interest in my quest.

The Amazon Exploration Series
Children's Books: by Constantine Issighos

1) Upper Amazon Voyage By River Boat
2) The People of the River
3) The Children of the River
4) Amazon's Nature of Things
5) Echoes of Nature: a Beautiful Wild Habitat
6) The Amazon Rainforest
7) Amazonian Sisterhood
8) Amazon River Wolves
9) Amazonian Landscapes and Sunsets
10) Amazonian Canopy: the Roof of the World's Rainforest
11) Amazonian Tribes: a World of Difference
12) Birds, Flowers and Butterflies of the Amazon
13) The Great Wonders of the Amazon
14) The Jaguar People
15) The Fresh Water Giants
16) The Call of the Shaman
17) Indigenous Families: Life in Harmony With Nature
18) Amazon in Peril
19) Giant Tarantulas and Centipes
20) The Amazon Ethnobotanical Garden
21) Amazon Warriors

OTHER BOOKS By: Constantine Issighos

1) The Magic World of In-Laid Pictorial Tapestries
2) For God, Country and Drug Prohibition
3) Prisoners of Our Ideals
4) How I Build My Six-Sited Log Home

The Gustave Eiffel Exploration Series

5) Gustave Eiffel: Beyond the Tower Vol. I
6) Gustave Eiffel: Genius of Iron Works Vol. II
7) Gustave Eiffel: Art of Metal Structures Vol. III

" The first principle of architectural beauty is the essential lines of a work shall be determined by the perfect functionality "

Alexandre Gustave Eiffel: 1832 - 1921

TABLE OF CONTENT
VOL. I

	Page
Sub-Title	1
Legal Page	2
Acknowledgements	3
Books by Constantine Issighos	4
Eiffel Quote	5

France
Exposition Universalle of 1889 7
Illustrations 12

US
Summary 35
Illustrations 38

México
MAP 87
Palacio de Orizaba
Summary 89
Illustrations 93

Church of Santa Barbara
Summary 152
Illustrations 155

Ecuador
MAP 199
Summary 201
Illustrations 203

Index 226

THE PARIS
EXPOSITION UNIVERSALLE 0f 1889

International expositions of commerce and industry were part of the Industrial Revolution's striving to demonstrate innovative success. Participants, through their exhibitions and pavilions, whether national or international, had one single intention: to show the world their own manufacturing, commercial and scientific capabilities. Wealthy nations such as France, Britain, Germany, Belgium and the USA had their large pavilions filled to capacity with national products ready to sell to potential customers.

Developing countries from South America, the French colonies and the Far East were there doing their best to show-off their agricultural and textile products. Competition among participants was fierce; each did its best to attract the attention of potential clients.

Not all exhibited products, however, could be housed within the restrictive space of a national pavilion. Engineering and construction firms from industrialized nations, for example, needed open air space to exhibit large iron structures intended for public lands in other countries. Bridges, churches and multi-purpose structures were exposed in allocated spaces within the compounds of the Exposition Universalle. Over eighty such iron structures were built on the Champ de Mars. Many of the achievements in engineering and architecture, the fine ornamental iron arts, and the new technologies were in the Exposition which was designed to highlight them.

Engineering firms who built machines for industrial, commercial or agricultural production were housed within special pavilions such as the impressive 1,452 foot-long Galerie des Machines designed by Ferdinard Dutert and Victor Contamin Perrion. Interested foreign visitors would take their time, question the vendors on the utility and performance of their machines, and arrange marine shipping to a chosen destination.

It was not all "business" at the Exposition Universalle of 1889. The History of Habitation exhibit provided an educational forum about human shelter in the French colonial villages. Exhibited dwellings were divided into three sectors: the pre-historic, historic and contemporary shelters. The Cacao van Hutten (Famous Coffee House) exhibited villagers in traditional Dutch dresses. Vietnamese actors and dancers exhibited their cultural performances, and the American soprano Sybil Sanderson attracted and entertained crowds of visitors for more than fifty evenings during the six months that the Exposition lasted. Straw hat makers from Indochina and the Caribbean demonstrated their unique skills. Miscellaneous exhibits included Thomas Edison's inventions and dioramas which were shown at the History of Work exhibit.

Most of the engineering and construction exhibitors at the Fair were French. Amongst them was Gustave Eiffel's company Construction CIE which participated with a number of prefabricated iron structures. These structures were temporarily assembled for the duration of the Fair. The aim was to entice costumers by the structural quality of the exhibited pre-assembled structures and their ornamental beauty. Small and large structures were for sale to anyone who could effort the price tag.

One of the Fair's visitors was Julius H. Toots, a rubber baron from the Upper Amazon city of Iquitos, Peru. Mr. Toots was so impressed with the size of the "Mansion" iron structure that he bought it while it was still part of the on-going exhibition. At the end of the Fair, the structure was disassembled, each support and ornamental part enumerated, nuts and bolts were packed in wooden boxes, and all was accompanied by the necessary blueprints. (For details see Casa de Fierro).

Most of the exhibited structures were built on "spec," meaning that they were built in the hope that a potential customer would be found to purchase it. Structures that were not bought at the Fair were removed and stored in Eiffel's warehouse facilities in France or Brussels.

Some of the exhibited iron structures were built in France as part of the Fair's exhibition, such as the Chilean Pavilion. It exhibited Chilean products for the duration of the Fair and then was dismantled and shipped to the Chilean capital of Santiago, where today it functions as the Museo Artequin. (For details see Museo Artequin.)

In 1896 Mr. LaForgue, Director of the French mining company Boleo of Baja California, was visiting Paris. He was familiar with Eiffel's style of structural and ornamental iron works and arranged to view one of the "specs" that could be used as a Catholic Church. After minor changes in the metallic structure, it was disassembled, enumerated, crated and shipped to Baja California. Today, the structure functions as the Santa Barbara Church and it is located in the mining town of Santa Rosalia. (For more details see Church of Santa Barbara.)

True enough, the name of Eiffel and his reputable works were well known amongst the various national and international engineering and construction firms. Eiffel's company in France was a forerunner in every aspect of engineering innovation. Winning the competition to build the Tower put him at the undisputed top level amongst his peers. But the general public knew very little about Eiffel's work and styles; that is, not until the Tower was put in place and served as the main entrance to the Fair. Newspaper articles about the Tower, some in favour and others against, were part of people's daily conversation.

The name "Eiffel" became known overnight. Structures made by Eiffel were now regarded as superior to all others. Orders were coming in as fast as could be accepted, resulting in the construction of hundreds of small, medium and large iron structures that were shipped all over Europe, Asia and South America. A number of ambitious politicians, businessmen and plutocrats wanted an "Eiffel" structure or monument to be part of their personal or political agenda. Cathedrals and churches that were designed and built by Eiffel were shipped to South American countries to become national places of worship.

To the delight of the French officials and the general public, a number of prominent visitors paid tribute to the engineers and architects who built the iron structures and pavilions exhibited at the Exposition Universalle. The list is long, but I shall mention just a few: Buffalo Bill, who recruited the American sharpshooter Annie Oakley—whom the polygamous king of Senegal attempted to purchase her for 100.000 francs-- to perform on his "Wild West Show" which delighted packed audiences throughout the Exposition; Vincent van Gogh, the renowned painter; the Prince of Wales (the future King Edward VII); the Filipino patriot Jose Rizal; and the inventor Thomas Edison.

The question still remains as to why this particular Exposition of 1889 is held to be something more than all the past and future European Expositions. Writers could speculate until "Hell freezes over." Some claim that it was because the Exposition Universalle of 1889 was visited by more than six and a half million visitors. Others put their emphasis on the exclusive structure and styles of national pavilions from around the world. Countless speculative opinions are available in books and tourist brochures. In my not-so-humble opinion, I say, "All of the above," plus the fact that in Europe of 1889 there was no other free-standing steel structure that was 300 meters tall with the unique body style of the Eiffel Tower. It afforded the first panoramic view of a clamorous city like Paris from such an altitude.

Equally significant a building-in both beauty and grace--constructed for the Fair was the Galerie des Machines. However, most of the colourful posters and brochures of the Fair had at their center the main advertising attraction--The Eiffel Tower. Even Eiffel complained later that his Tower was more famous than he was. Did the presence of the Eiffel Tower undermine the importance of the Exposition Universalle itself? Not at all, because the Fair's main theme and emphasis was the technological aspect of innovative engineering and architecture, and the Eiffel Tower had both--the presence of an innovative structural technology and entertainment for the general public.

In addition to its technological aspects, the Fair was also about the cultural differences and ethno-diversity amongst its participants:

The Pagoda of Angkor served as the main entrance to the Javanese Village. The structure came directly from Java, as did the popular Javanese dancers whose performance expressed their cultural tradition.

The cultural Pavilion of Cochin-China represented the French colony which along with Annan and Tonkin, later became Vietnam.
The Pavilion of Annan and Tonkin represented the French protectorate, which, along with Cambodia, Laos and Cochin-China were part of the Federation that formed Indochina.

The African Pavilion consisted of a "village" of 43 small dwellings which were constructed to represent the cultural styles of various African epochs and cultures.

The Pavilion of Venezuela represented a highly sculptural Spanish cultural style, featuring the national colours of yellow, red and blue.

The Pavilion of Brazil was built in a neo-Portuguese nautical style representing the rivers of Brazil and its immense agricultural resources, including rubber-latex, chocolate and vanilla beans, sugar cane and indigenous handcrafts.

In short, the Exposition Universalle of 1889 exhibited various liberal arts including archaeology, anthropology, astronomy, chemistry, physics, medicine, theatre, as well as transportation and the military arts.

1889 BRAZILIAN PAVILION

1889-BOLIVIAN PAVILION

1889 PANORAMIC VIEW OF EIFFEL TOWER

1889-PANORAMIC VIEW OF THE FAIR
AND THE EIFFEL TOWER

1889-A VIEW FROM WITHIN

Exposition Universalle of 1889

1889-A PANORAMIC VIEW OF PARIS

POST CARD CIRCA-1889

1889-CENTRAL DOME, GALLERY DES MACHINES

THE EIFFEL EXPLORATION SERIES — Constantine Issighos

1889-AFRICAN VILLAGERS

1889-PAVILION OF FRENCH COLONIES

1889-CAIRO STREET

THE EIFFEL EXPLORATION SERIES   Constantine Issighos

1889-PAVILION COCHIN CHINA

1889-PAVILION OF DANGKIR

Exposition Universalle of 1889

1889-CENTRAL DOME-GALERRY DES MACHINES

1889-POSTER OF EIFFEL TOUR

1889-PAVILION OF CHINA

1889-PAVILION OF ARGENTINE

1889-ENTRANCE TO THE FAIR

1889-TONGUINOIS PAVILION

EIFFEL TOWER IRON WORKERS IN 1889

1889 EXPOSITION UNIVERSALLE

STATE OF EIFFEL TOWER CONSTRUCTION DURING THE INITIAL DAYS OF THE FAIR 1889

Exposition Universalle of 1889

Exposition Universalle of 1889

THE EIFFEL EXPLORATION SERIES Constantine Issighos

Exposition Universalle of 1889

1889-PANORAMIC VIEW OF THE DOME DES MACHINES

1889-DOME DES MACHINES (CLOSE-UP)

1889-GALLERT OF ARTS

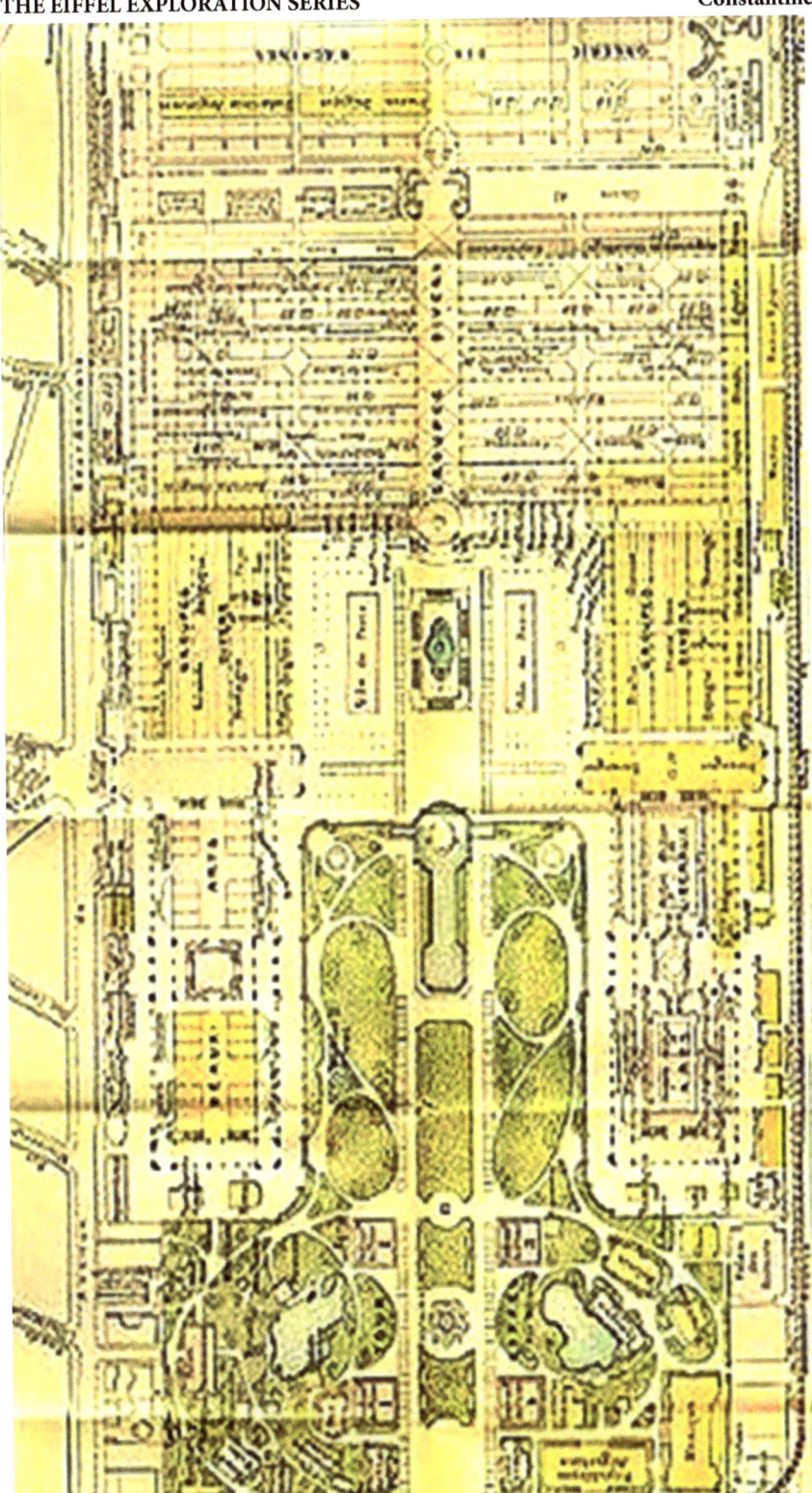

Exposition Universalle of 1889

THE EIFFEL EXPLORATION SERIES　　　　　　　　　　Constantine Issighos

1889-INTERIOR OF THE GALLERY DES MACHINES

1889-POST CARD OF THE GALLERY DES MACHINES

Exposition Universalle of 1889

POSTER COMMEMORATING THE 100 ANNIVERSARY OF THE STORM OF BASTILLE

STATUTE OF LIBERTY

THE SUPPORT SYSTEM OF THE STATUTE OF LIBERTY

In a span of fifty years—1880 - 1930—more than 23 million new immigrants saw, for the first time, the Statute of Liberty as they entered the Port of New York. For many, the sight of the Statute of Liberty was the gateway to the American Dream. The lawless city of New York offered opportunities to many and great wealth for the few.

The new frontiers drew rural migrants and newly arrived immigrant workers. The millions flocking to urban areas often experienced overcrowded neighbourhoods and diseased-redden tenements. Against this terrible reality there stood the statute's torch and a tabula ansata—a tablet evoking the law—reminding all that this is the land of the free.

I first thought of dedicate this brief article on pure technical aspects of the Statute's structural support system. It would have involved technical details with narrow scope. I had therefore a choice to bore the reader with such details or describe—tell a story—the statute's outer parts that are fastened to the core pylon support system. I chose the later and also because the core pylon and its support system are mostly covered by the Statute's copper skin which eliminates a visual variation.

My research led me to various public archives and private sources showing the original plaster moulds of the various parts of the Statute as were put together in the studio of Auguste Bartholdi—its designer—that would fastened onto Eiffel's support system. It also led me to collect photos of the actual construction work and the assembling of the Statute's copper skin.

When the Stature of Liberty's initial structural designer Eugene Viollet-le-Duc died suddenly in 1879, the Franco-American Union and Auguste Bertholdi hired Gustave Eiffel as his replacement. While Eiffel praised Viollet-le-Duc original structural designed he ultimately adopted his own, a much more advance structural support system. The new support system would not rely on the weight of the statute's 100 tons copper skin, but rather on a free standing pylon support system.

Eiffel designed a 93 foot high wrought iron square core pylon whose structural members were four posts to work in conjunction to other parts. The core pylon supports an outer secondary iron skeleton frame, that is, it carries a system of flat iron bars where the copper plates would hang-on (or screwed-on) to and which would form the statute's exterior skin. On the upper level of the core pylon; and extending from it, there are smaller flat-bar frames that supporting the statute's head. A slim arm-pylon of 47- 7in long would be carrying the arm-structure that holds the statute's torch.

The Statute's body is internally braced onto diagonal flat-bars which are designed to withstand a wind load of 58 psf (pressure per square-foot) on 50 miles-mph wind. In such a case the statute moves either way up to 3-in.

Once Eiffel's design was approved by the Franco-American Union and Auguste Bartholdi, Eiffel travelled to U.S.A. to supervise the construction of the statute's structural support system until its completion in November 1883.

"LADY LIBERT" IN PARIS - BEFORE BEING SHIPPED TO NEW YORK

THE INNOVATIVE CREATORS OF THE STATUTE OF LIBERTY

FINAL TOUCHES ON STATUTE'S TORCH

ILLUSTRATOR'S CONCEPT OF STATUTE'S BASE

ADJUSTING THE STATUTE'S FLAMES

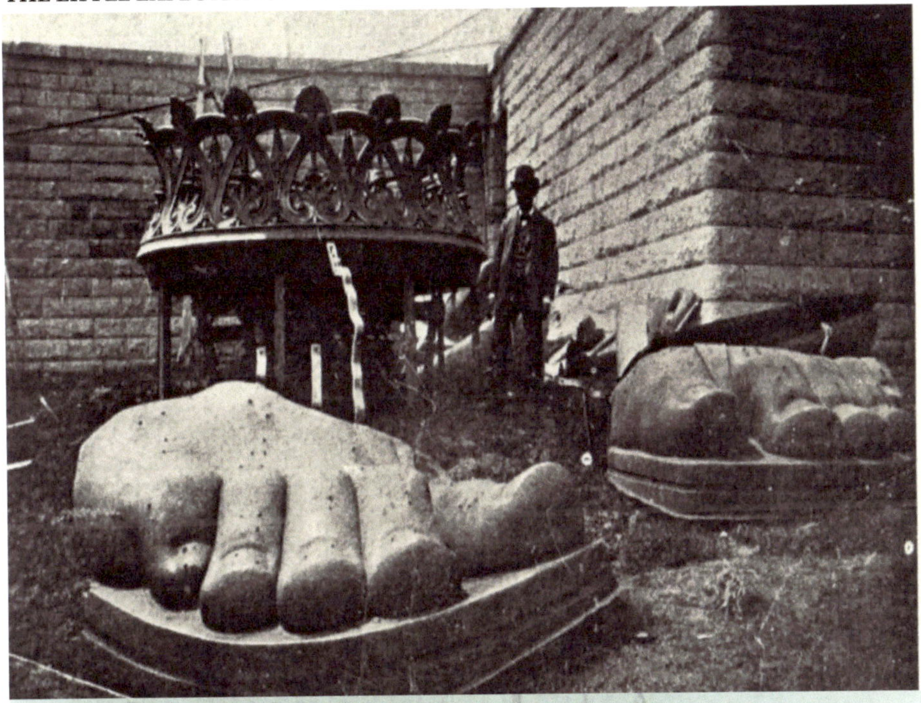

A PLACE TO REST THE STATUTE'S FEET

THE EIFFEL EXPLORATION SERIES Constantine Issighos

FROM PLASTER MOULD TO COPPER SKIN

MAIN SPIRAL STAIRS WITH EXTENDED
SUPPORT SYSTEM

THE EIFFEL EXPLORATION SERIES   Constantine Issighos

STUDIO WORK IN PROGRESS

Statute Of Liberty

CORE PYLON SUPPORT SYSTEM

THE STATUTE'S CORE SUPPORT SYSTEM

THE EIFFEL EXPLORATION SERIES — Constantine Issighos

**PHOTO OF MADAM BERTHOLDI IN THE
INITIAL STATE OF HEAD´S PREPARATION**

STATUTE´S WORK IN PROGRESS

STATUTE OF LIBERTY

STATUTE´S PANORAMIC VIEW

STUDIO WORK SCENES

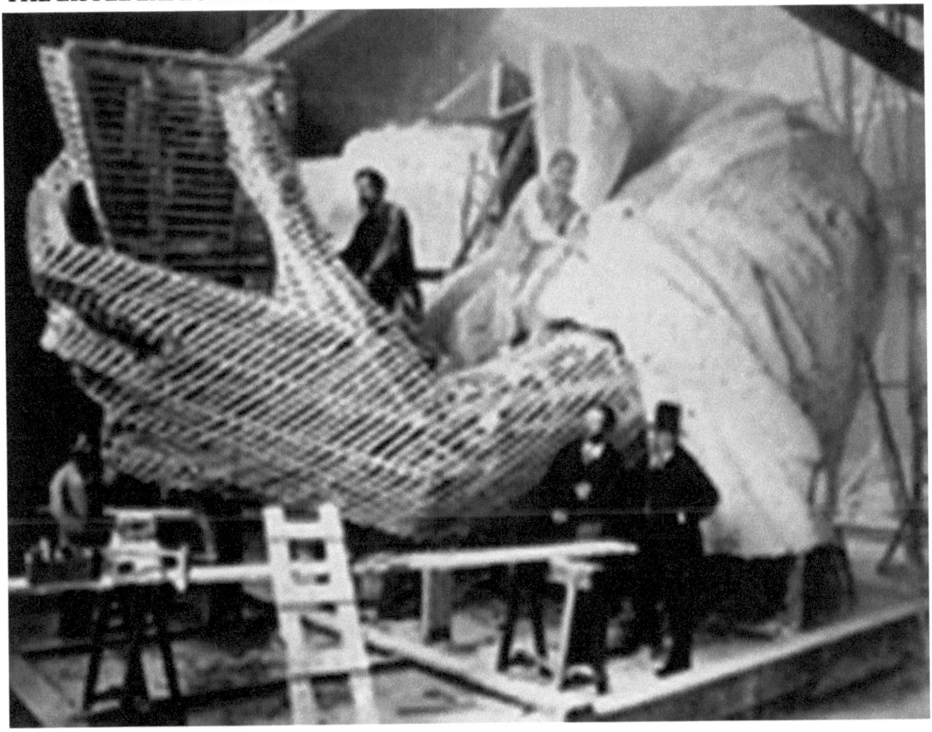

STUDIO WORKS ON STATUTE'S ARM AND HAND

FINISHING WORK ON STATUTE"S UPPER BODY

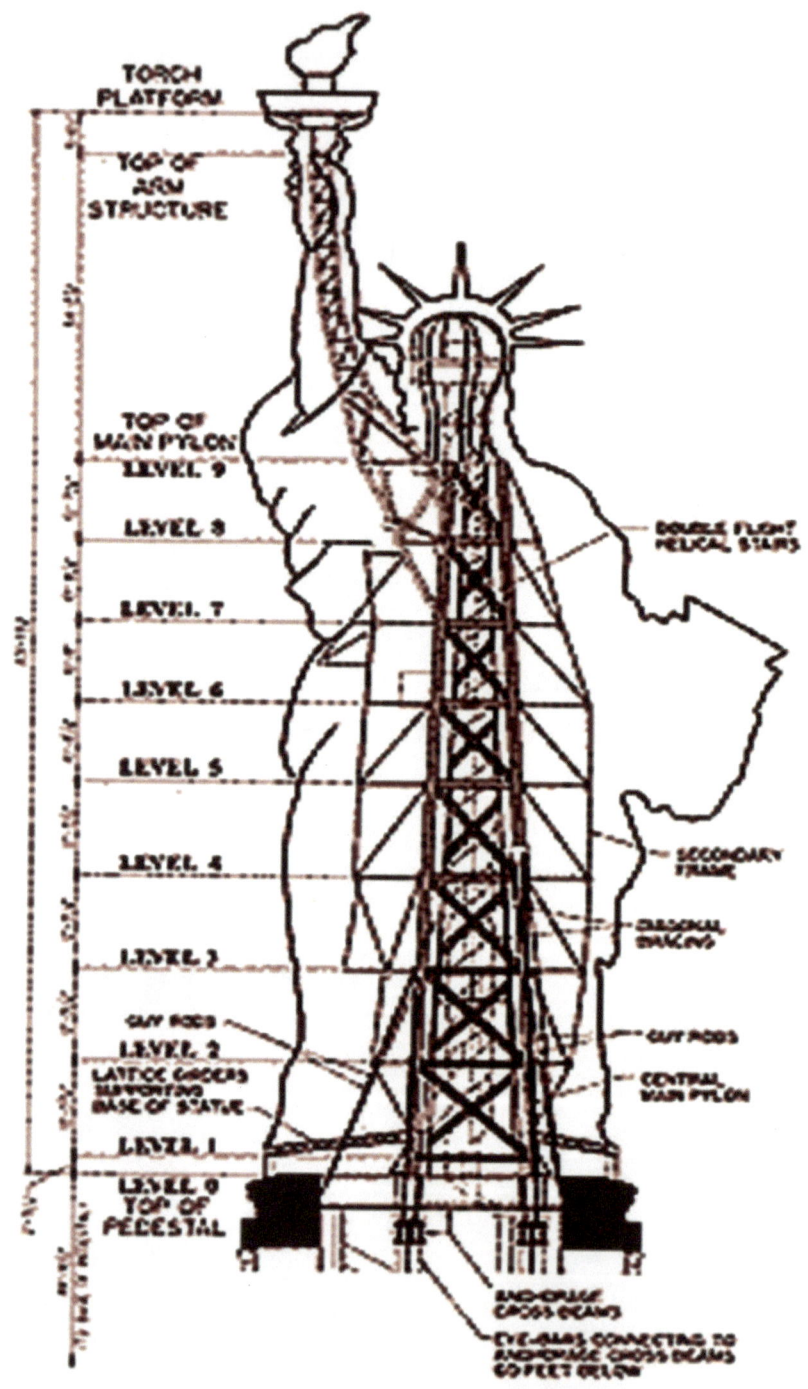

STATUTE OF LIBERTY ARCHITECTURAL DRAWING OF CORE PYLON SUPPORT SYSTEM

Statute Of Liberty

INTERNAL CONSTRUCTION

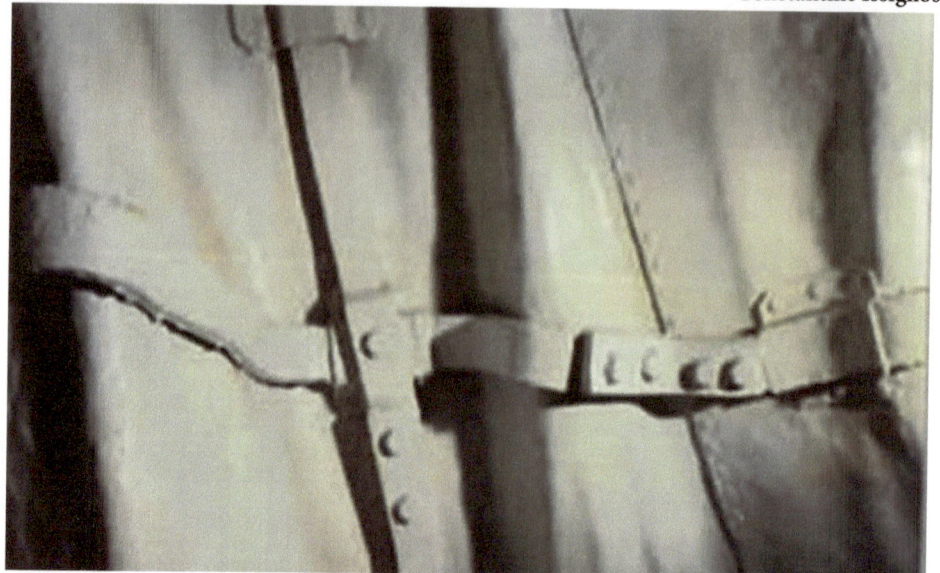

MODEL OF SUPPORT SYSTEM

THE EIFFEL EXPLORATION SERIES — Constantine Issighos

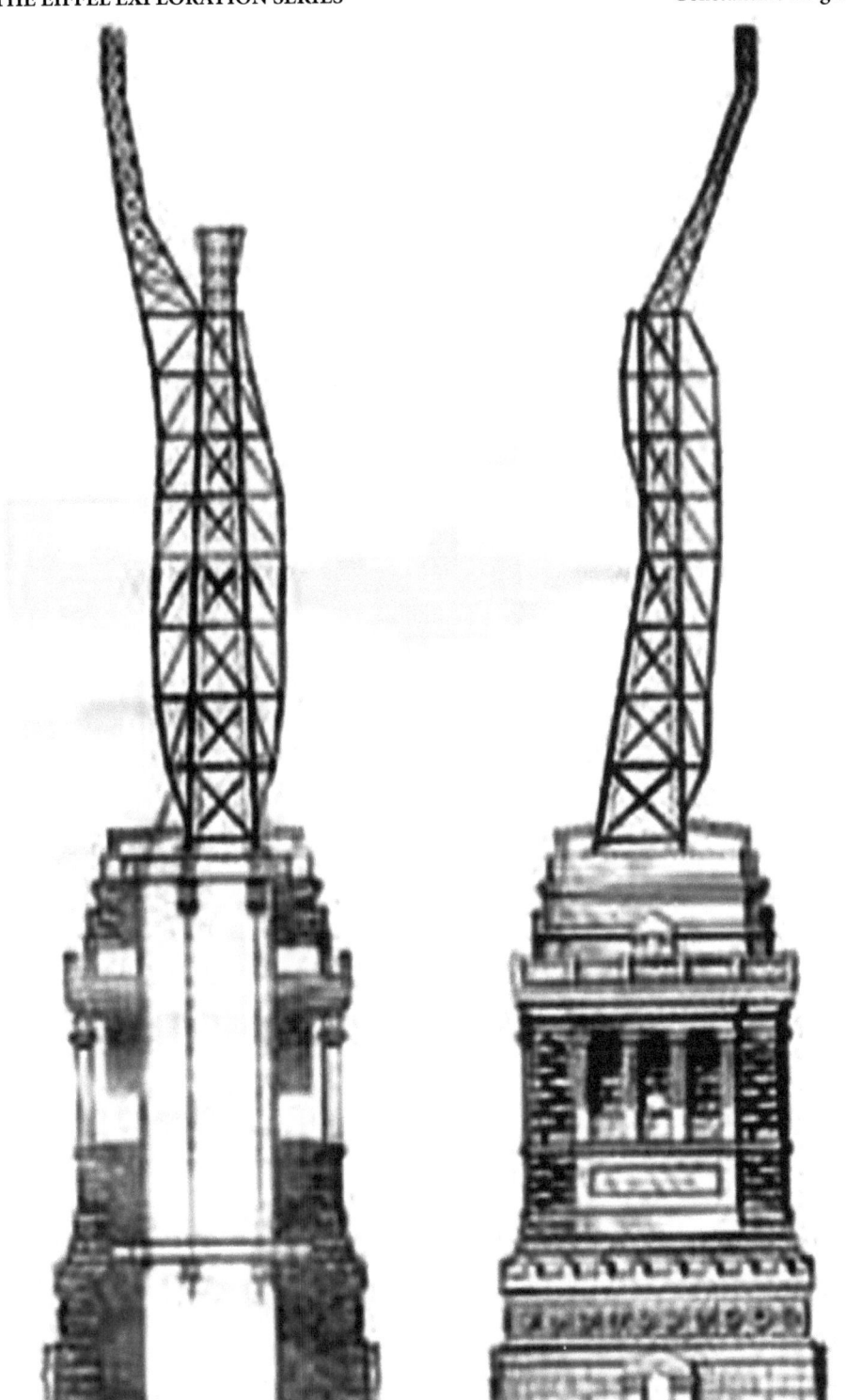

STATUTE OF LIBERTY SUPPORT SYSTEM

THE EIFFEL EXPLORATION SERIES — Constantine Issighos

Statute Of Liberty

THE EIFFEL EXPLORATION SERIES   Constantine Issighos

Statute Of Liberty

THE EIFFEL EXPLORATION SERIES   Constantine Issighos

Statute Of Liberty

THE EIFFEL EXPLORATION SERIES   Constantine Issighos

Statute Of Liberty

THE EIFFEL EXPLORATION SERIES — Constantine Issighos

Statute Of Liberty

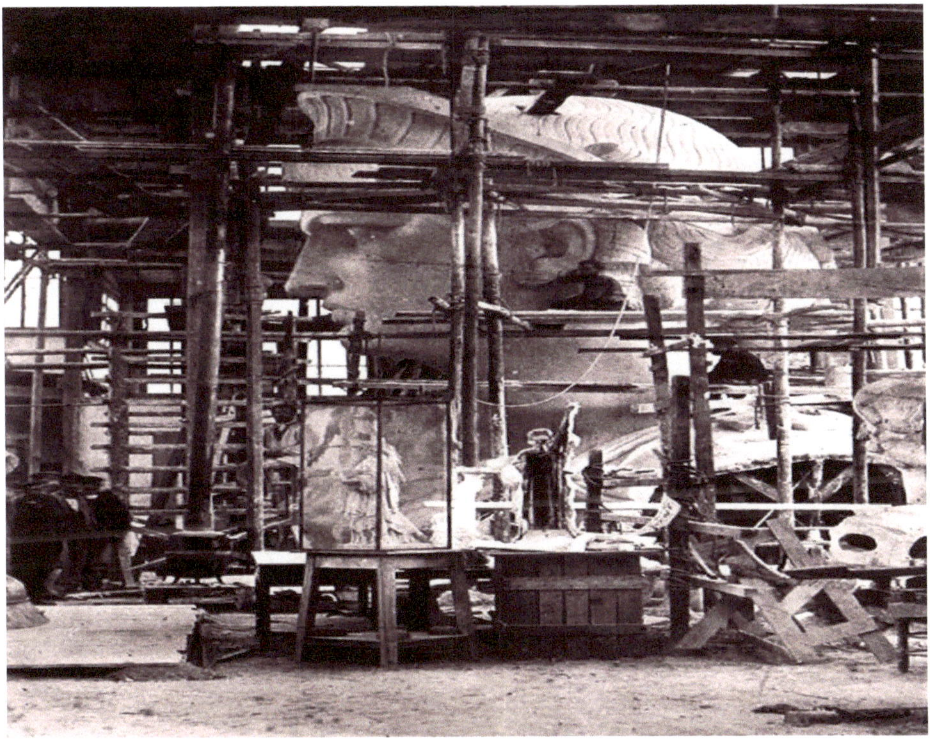

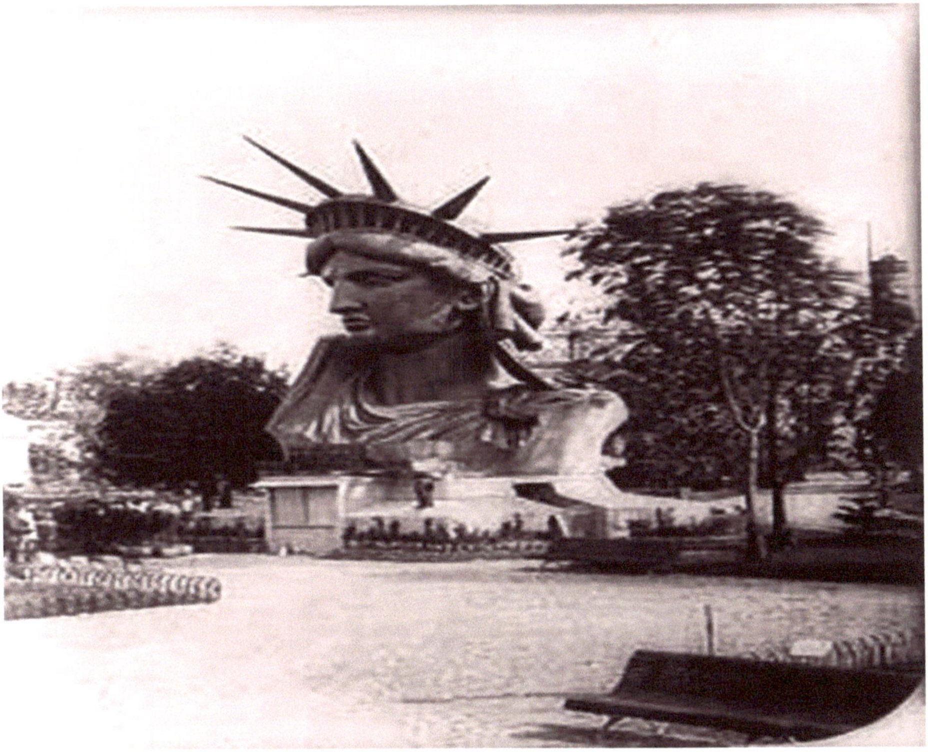

THE EIFFEL EXPLORATION SERIES   Constantine Issighos

Statute Of Liberty

Statute Of Liberty

THE EIFFEL EXPLORATION SERIES — Constantine Issighos

Statute Of Liberty

THE EIFFEL EXPLORATION SERIES   Constantine Issighos

                                                        Statute Of Liberty

Statue Of Liberty

THE EIFFEL EXPLORATION SERIES   Constantine Issighos

Statute Of Liberty

THE EIFFEL EXPLORATION SERIES
Constantine Issighos

Statute Of Liberty

Statute Of Liberty

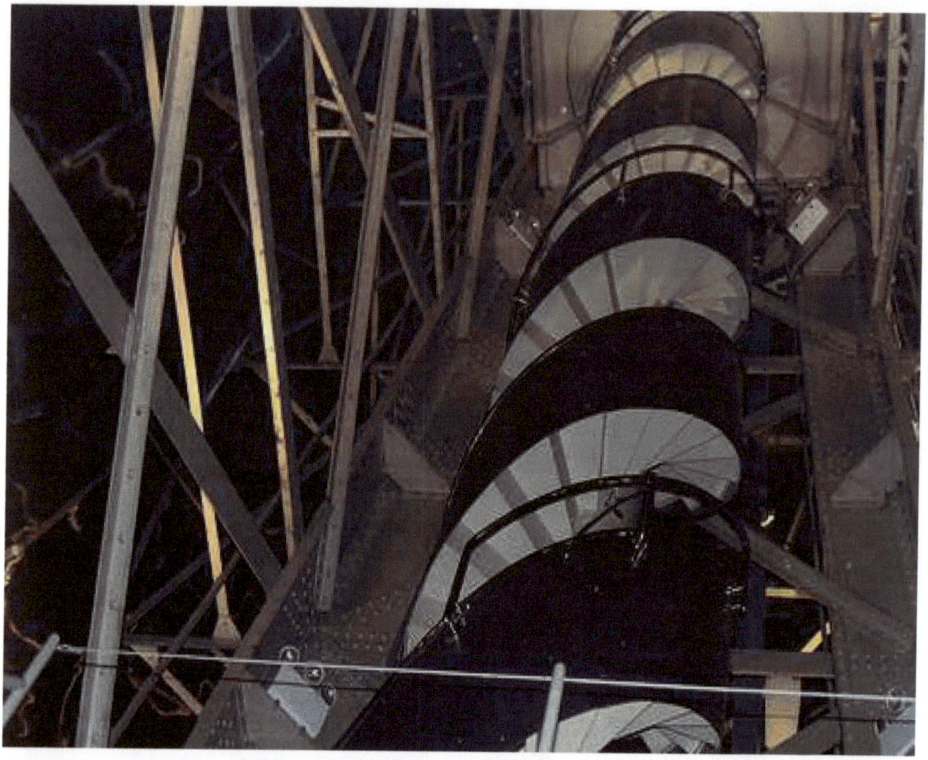

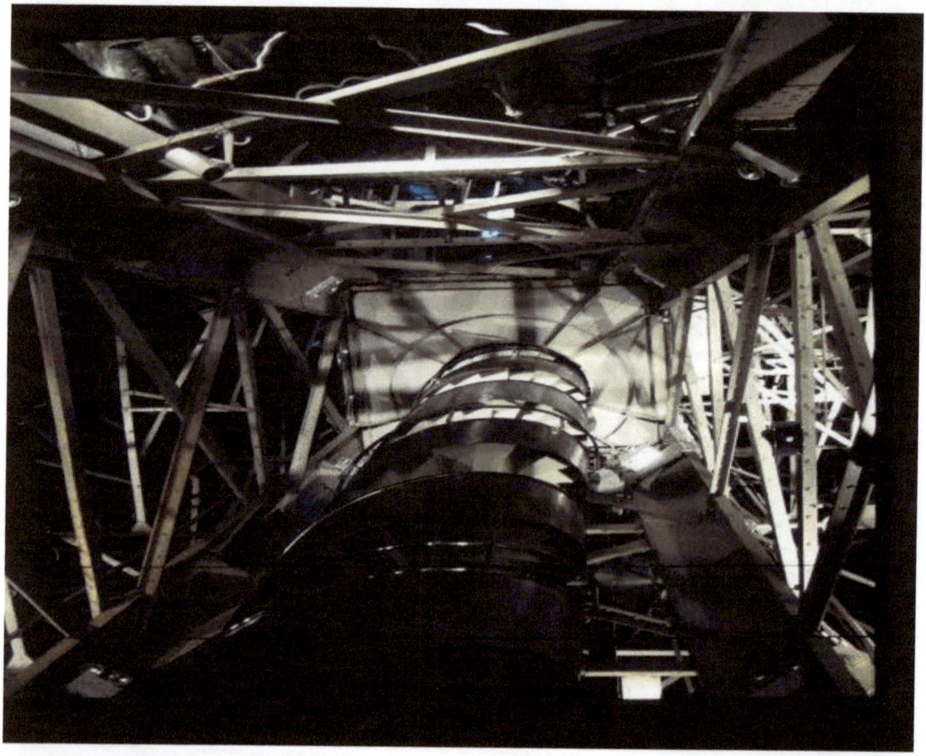

THE EIFFEL EXPLORATION SERIES   **Constantine Issighos**

Statute Of Liberty

THE EIFFEL EXPLORATION SERIES — Constantine Issighos

Statute Of Liberty

THE EIFFEL EXPLORATION SERIES　　　　　　　　　　　　　Constantine Issighos

Statute Of Liberty

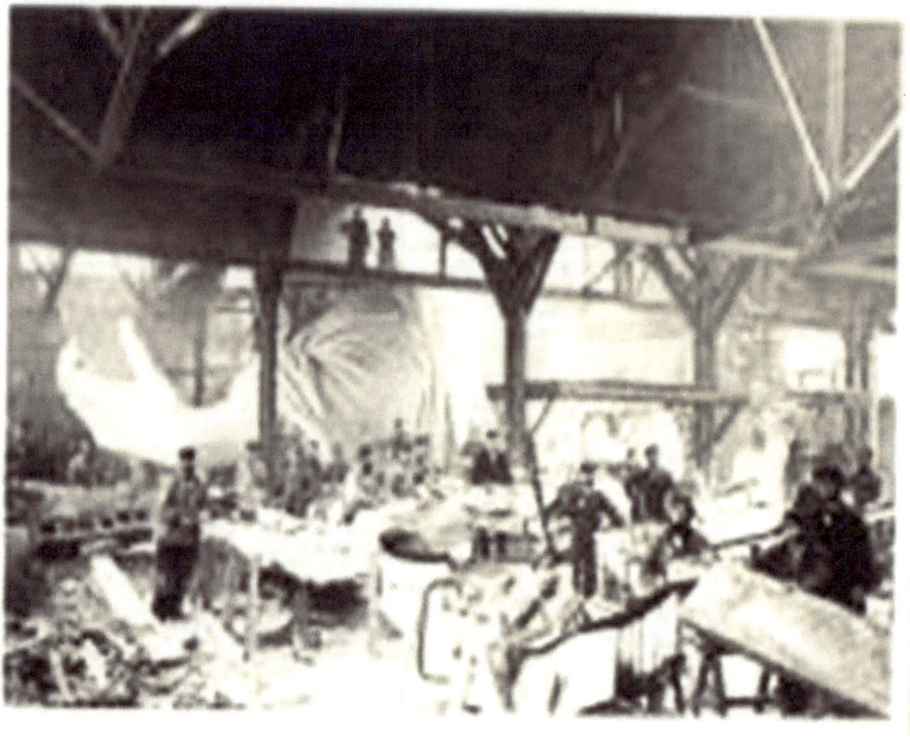

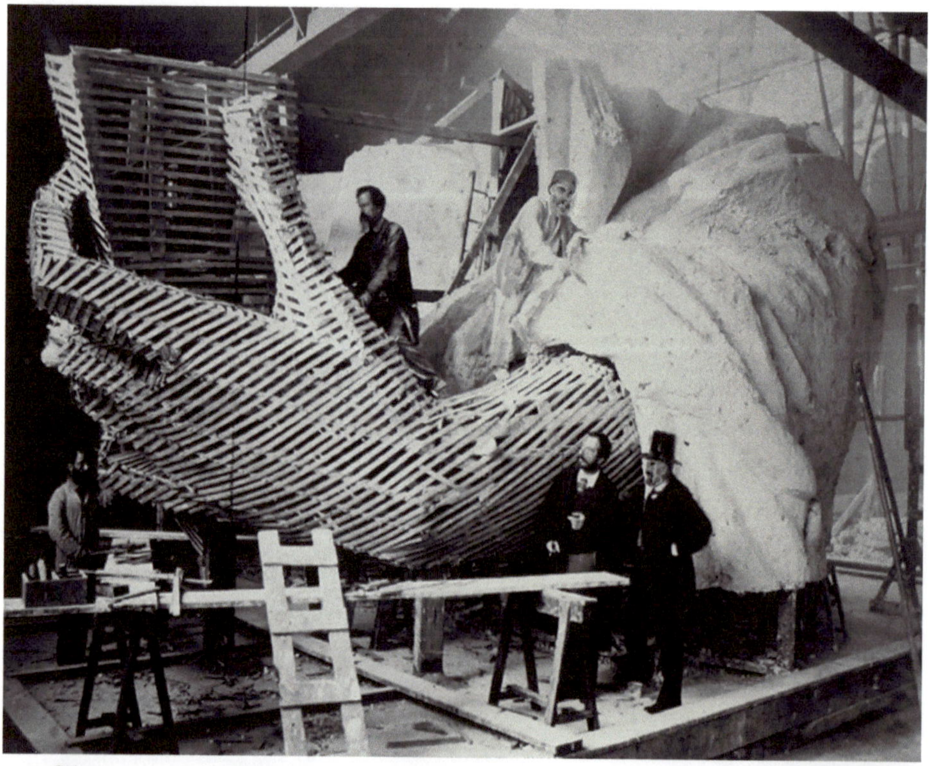

THE EIFFEL EXPLORATION SERIES Constantine Issighos

Palacio de Hierro

EL PALACIO DE HIERRO

EL PALACIO DE HIERRO

The city of Orizaba, in the state of Veracruz, Mexico, became the hometown of early Spanish settlers in 1521. It was important at the time of the Spanish conquest because of its established trade route facilities. During the colonial conquest, Orizaba became an important port city in the service of Spain for the transportation of soldiers, wealth and general goods on their way to the motherland. On January 27, 1774, the Spanish King Carlos III conceded a town status to Orizaba, and on November 29, 1830, Orizaba was declared a city.

By the end of the 1800s, Orizaba was considered the most culturally advanced city in Mexico, its fourth most important trade city and the city with the most highly educated people. Due to this, a large number of foreigners were attracted to Orizaba, including Greek, Italian, French, German, English, American, Swedish and Spanish settlers to establish new ventures and commercial enterprises. Most of them were there to try their luck and make their fortune. Each ethnic influx brought a distinct cultural flavour and customs as well as the latest trends in European fashion and architecture. Of course, the "international" city of Orizaba had a distinctly French feel to it.

On Sept. 25, 1891, Orizaba's Mayor Julio M. Velez, with popular support and desiring to distinguish the city, placed an order with the Belgian Societe Anonime des Forges D' Aiseau to construct an exceptional building that would represent the unique modernity and financial status of Orizaba. The building would showcase Orizaba's international character to the world and become a proud cultural symbol for Orizaba and the state of Veracruz.

The Belgian company offered the project to be designed by the most celebrated and innovative civil engineer of Europe, Alexandre Gustave Eiffel. The enormous success of the Exposition Universalle of 1889, visited by more than 6 million visitors, was a great triumph for Eiffel and his unique ornamental style of iron construction using pre-fabricated original techniques.

It was originally ordered and designed with the intention of housing the Government's Headquarters for the city. It was built with 600 hundred tons of Belgian steel; its prefabricated parts were shipped from Belgium during the government of Porfirio Diaz to be reassembled in Orizaba. It appears that while the government of the day had no money in its coffers to pay for the entire cost of the Palacio de Hierro, it was Don Manuel Carillo Tablas who loaned the money to the city. He also had to pay the additional cost for unloading the structure at the port and having it reassembled at its present location in the Plaza de Armas (Civic Square). Unfortunately, Senor Tablas died in 1899 without ever receiving a cent in repayment from the city.

The noted Mexican cultural historian Monja Alferez, in a 2009 article, described in detail the journey of the Palacio de Hierro:

"The cost [of the Palacio de Hierro] was in excess of 71,000 in gold Pesos, mainly supported by the grand loan the illustrious philanthropist and Orizaba's native son Sr Don Manuel Carrillo Tablas. The rest was covered by the State and by the Municipality as well."

Once the iron structure was completed, it was shipped to its destination:

"The complete cargo (3369 boxes plus the metallic structure) was shipped to the Port of Vera-cruz from Antwerp in 3 separated steamships: the Pans, the Vala and the Haver. At their arrival to Vera-cruz, the cost of the unloading and transportation to Orizaba's mountains required of 10,000 pesos more, which it was covered, once again, by the city's patron, Sr Carrillo Tablas. The hi[sic] cost of construction proposed by the Belgian company forced the city to employ only the structure's blueprints to assemble the giant metal palace."

All the crates containing the metal structural and ornamental parts, including the thousands of nuts and bolts, were finally unloaded. There was still the next step to be taken: the actual ground construction and the assembling of the pre-fabricated metal sections of the building. This was a challenge, for the local workers had no experience in assembling pre-fabricated structures by following numbers, letters and blueprint instructions.

"...The City hired a team of Mexican Architects and ....workers. The team was commanded by Mexican engineers, Arturo B. Boca (foundations) and Ricardo Segura (construction). The assigned [building] lot was the city's old Army Plaza in between the City Hall and the current Municipal House (present-- Alvarez Zardain Building). The old trees that embellished the plaza for centuries were transplanted to the Alameda. The grand inauguration was held on the eve of September 16, 1894 along with the festivities of Mexico's Independence....exactly one year after its construction started."

From its inauguration day, the Palacio de Hierro functioned as the city's Municipal Hall until 1991. Thereafter, various cultural and civic bodies used its elegant space, such as the Museum of Archaeology, a Library, an Office of Tourism and a Coffee Shop. Much of the surrounded landscape has been reasonably maintained as part of the government's efforts to preserve the city's cultural and ecological heritage.

Most of Eiffel's iron structures in the Americas are in urgent need of maintenance. After years of neglect, the Art Nouveau metallic structure of the Palacio de Hierro is in great need of special attention to preserve this world-class architectural jewel.

Legend has it that the Palacio de Hierro is one of the ten most important engineering achievements of Gustave Eiffel. Some countries where Eiffel's metal structures are located have declared them to be "National Treasures," thus preventing any major alterations or their destruction. I hope that one day soon, the Palacio de Hierro of the city of Orizaba, in the state of Veracruz, Mexico, will be recognized for its cultural and historical importance.

Recently, I revisited the Palacio de Hierro and to my pleasant surprise there were many structural improvements done in its exterior and interior. While I was there, I noticed the extensive electrical work done to illuminate the column system of its exterior. I expressed my personal gratitude to the Director Ing. Ricardo Rodriguez Demeneghi for the extensive improvements that were done on such important Eiffel monument. In the next several days, I was given a cultural tour of the Palacio de Hierro and was also taken to the City Archives to review original documents pertaining the ordering of the metal structure. The space of the Palacio de Hierro is occupied by:

The Museo Interactivo de Orizaba (Interacting Museum of Orizaba) houses various aspects of Science and Technology in an educational format.

The Museo de las Raises de Orizaba (Museum of ancient Races of Orizaba) demonstrates the historical roots of various indigenous populations, their prehistoric dress ware, environmental & cultivating tools and ethnic diversity.

The Museo de Futebol (The Sport Museum of Football) dedicates various drawing showing the origins of the sport in Orizaba, antique uniforms, trophies, banners and historic photographs.
In the Museo de Cerveza (Museum of Beer Making) shows the water quality of Valley of Orizaba which became the primary element for the evolutionary success of the local beer industry since 1894.

In the Planetario Rodouro Neri Vela (Planetarium of Rodouro Neri Vela) houses various models of the solar planetary system and commemorates the first Mexican astronaut who participated in space exploration.

In the Museo de Banderas (Museum of National Flags) deals with Mexican national identity during historical stages in the development of its national flag.

In the Museo de Presidentes Y Constiticiones (Museum of pass Presidents and Constitutions) deals with the history of the Republic of Mexico through the images of its presidents and constitutions.
Finally, I was very impressed by the courteous professionalism of the staff and their willingness to take visitors through every aspect of the Palacio de Hierro.

SIDE VIEW OF THE PALACE

GARDEN VIEW OF THE PALACE

DETAILS OF FRONTAL VIEW

ARCHIVE PHOTOGRAPHS

THE EIFFEL EXPLORATION SERIES   Constantine Issighos

Palacio de Hierro

PHOTO CIRCA 1930

PHOTO CIRCA 1940's

Palacio de Hierro

THE EIFFEL EXPLORATION SERIES — Constantine Issighos

100 — Palacio de Hierro

THE EIFFEL EXPLORATION SERIES   Constantine Issighos

Palacio de Hierro

CELEBRATING LOCAL THEMES

THE EIFFEL EXPLORATION SERIES　　　　　　　　　　　Constantine Issighos

104　　　　　　　　　　　　　　　　　　　　　　　　Palacio de Hierro

THE EIFFEL EXPLORATION SERIES　　　　　　　　　　Constantine Issighos

AUTHOR IN THE CLOCK TOWER

Palacio de Hierro

THE EIFFEL EXPLORATION SERIES — Constantine Issighos

INTERIOR METAL PARTITIONS

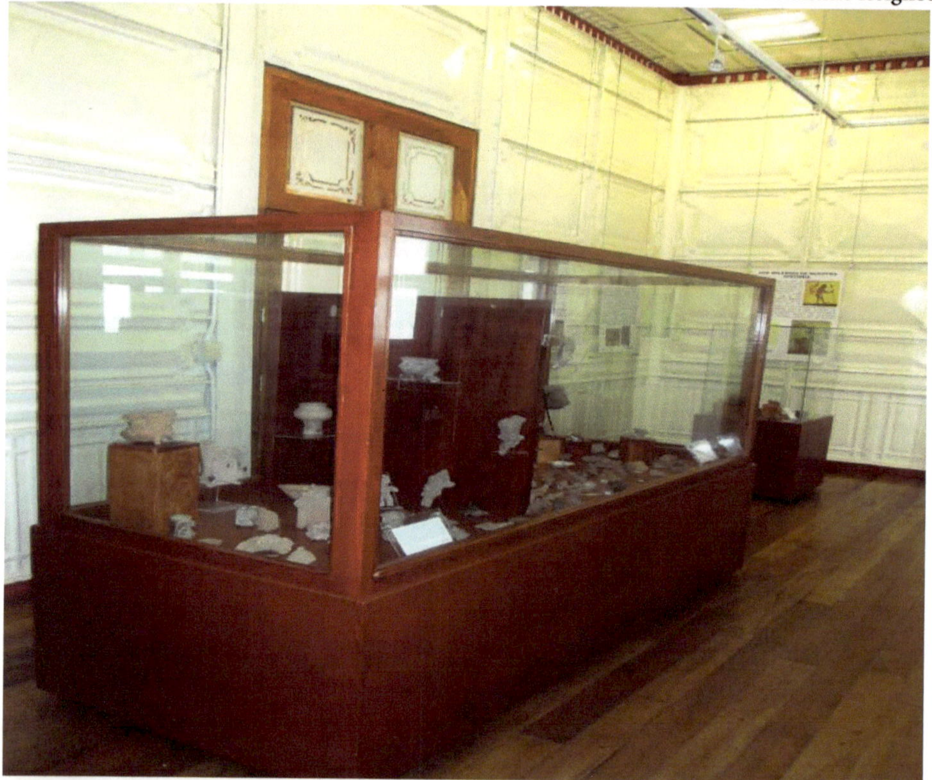

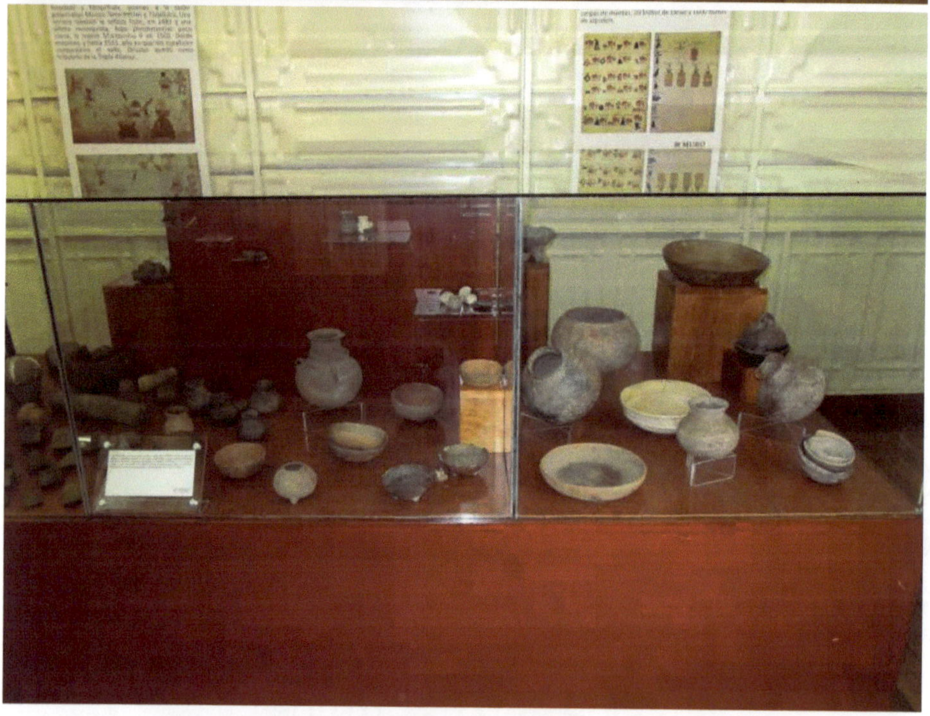

REGIONAL ARCHEOLOGICAL ARTIFACTS

THE EIFFEL EXPLORATION SERIES   Constantine Issighos

Palacio de Hierro

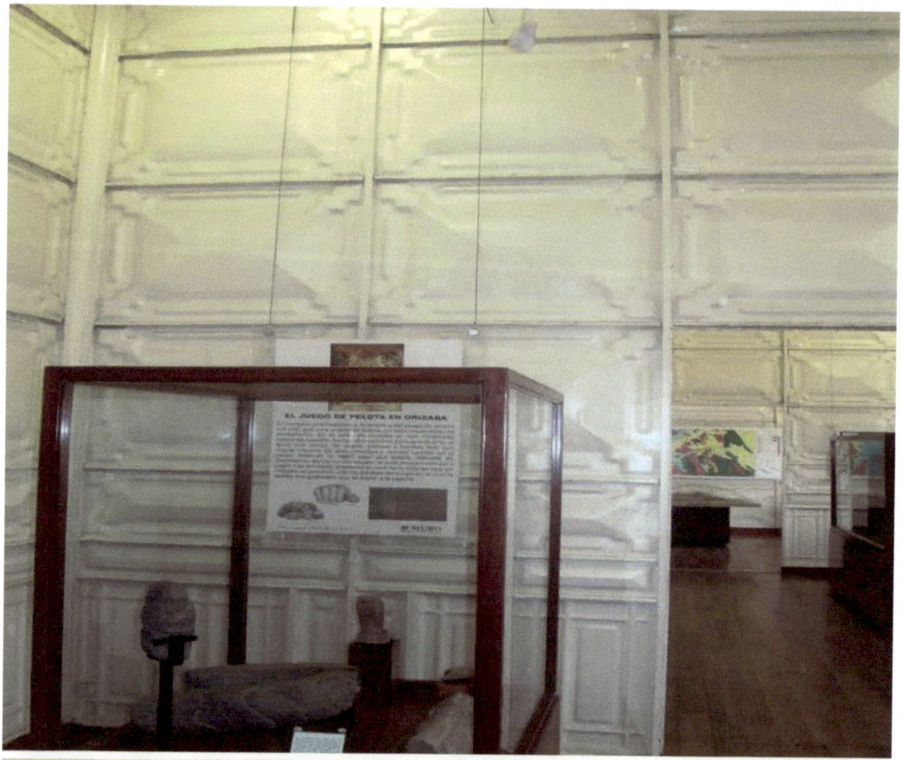
EL JUEGO DE PELOTA EN ORIZABA

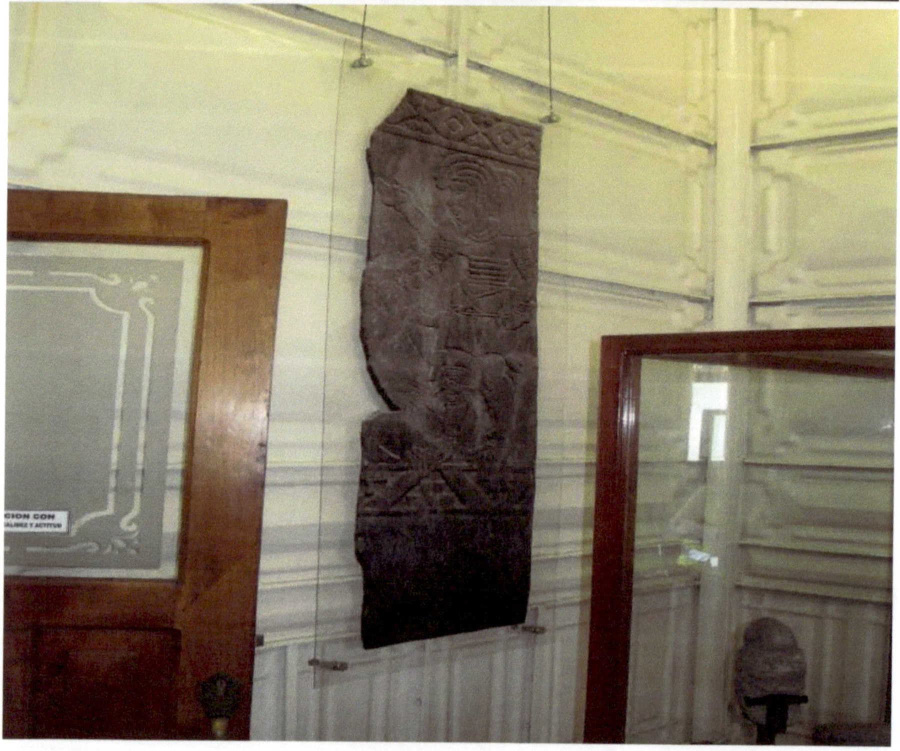

MUSEUM OF MEXICO'S PAST PRESIDENTS

THE EIFFEL EXPLORATION SERIES Constantine Issighos

Palacio de Hierro

SPACE MUSEUM

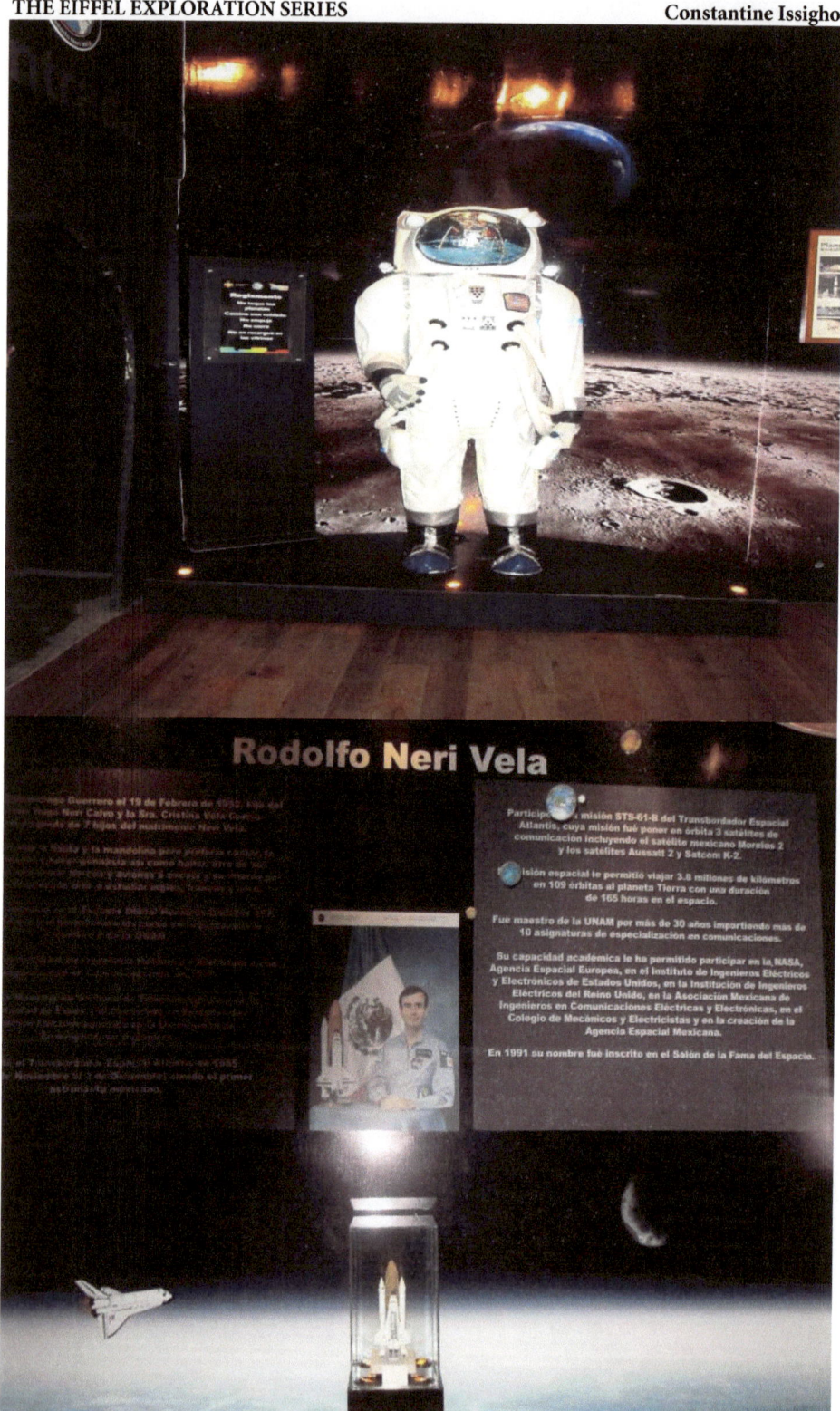

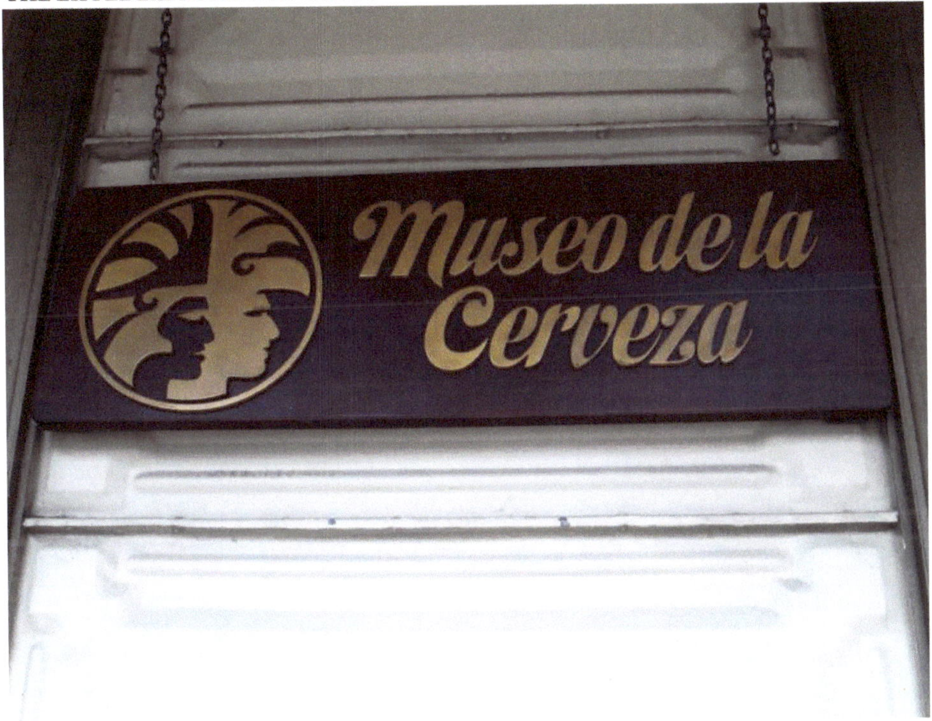
Museo de la
Cerveza

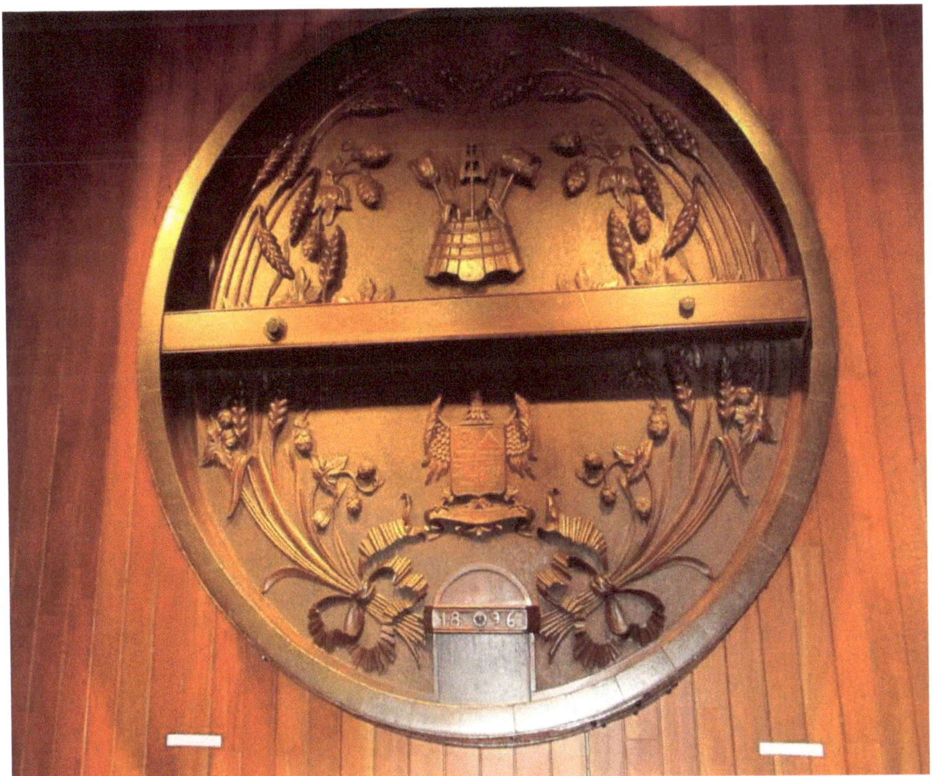

Palacio de Hierro

MUSEUM OF LOCAL INDIGENOUS POPULATION

CELEBRATING WORKS OF LOCAL ARTISTS

CELEBRATING FIRST SETTLERS IN THE AREA

CELEBRATING THE ORIGEN OF SOCCER

METAL PARTITIONS STYLE CHARACTERISTIC OF EIFFEL

Palacio de Hierro

THE EIFFEL EXPLORATION SERIES   Constantine Issighos

Palacio de Hierro

A BALCONY COFFEE SHOP SERVES VISITORS

VIEWING ORIGINAL DOCUMENTS AT MUNICIPAL RECORDS

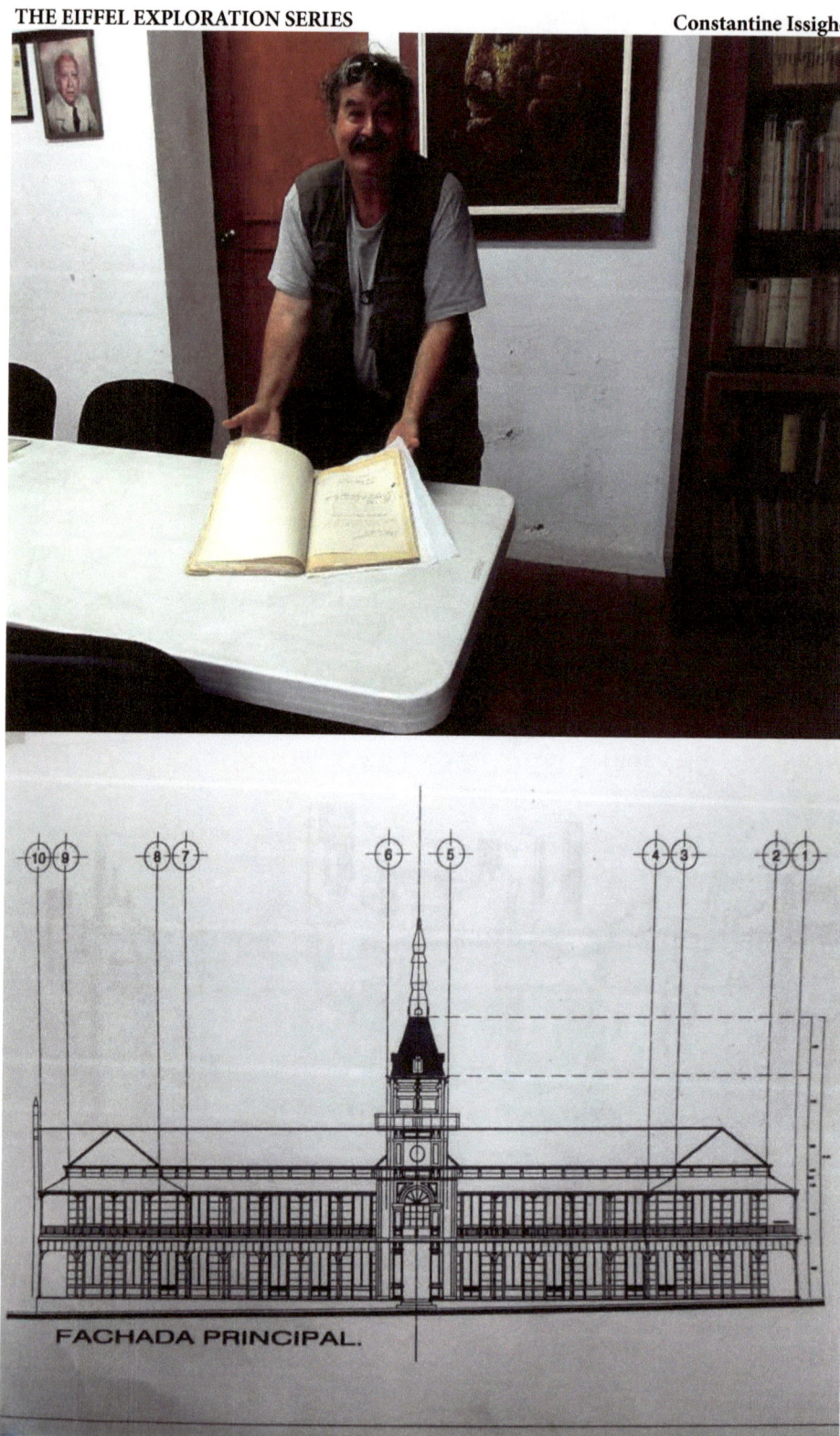

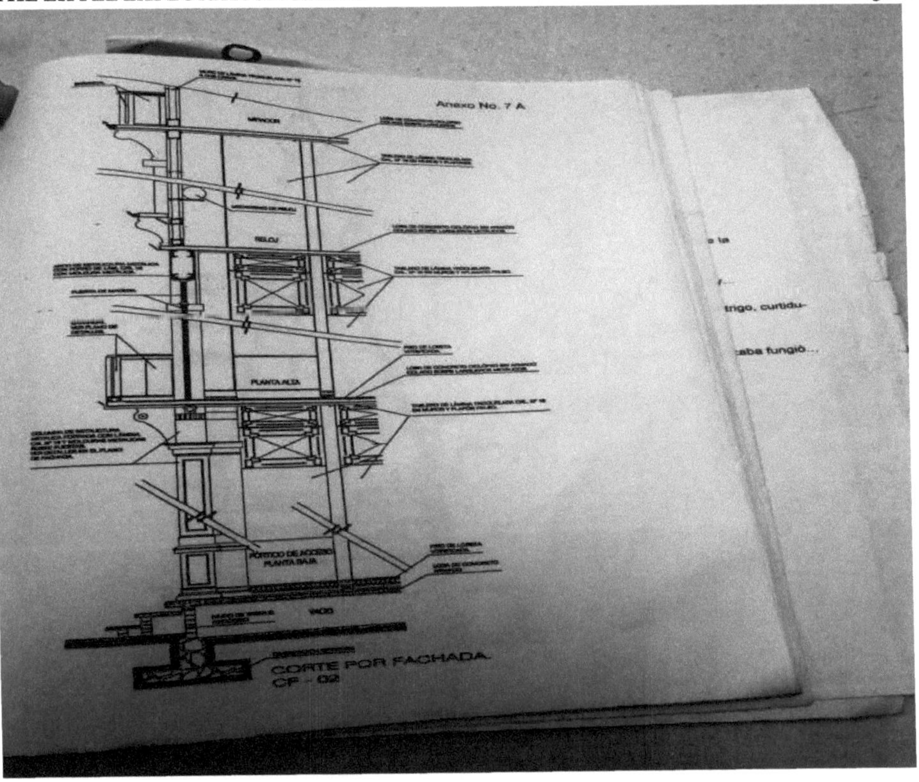

THE EIFFEL EXPLORATION SERIES

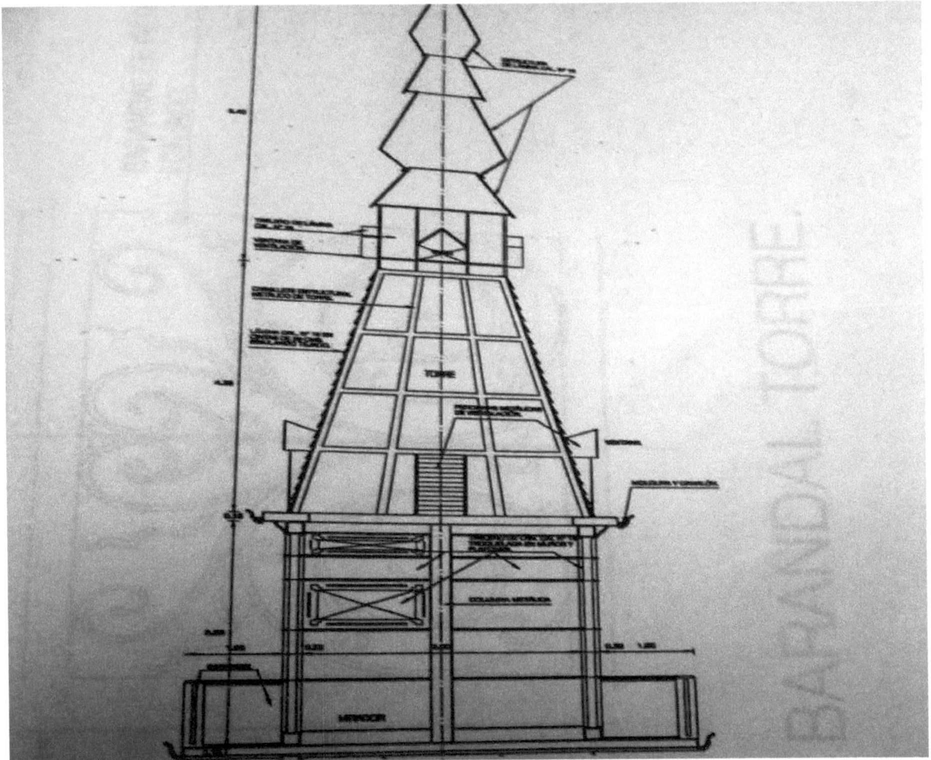

Columna Exterior Planta Baja.

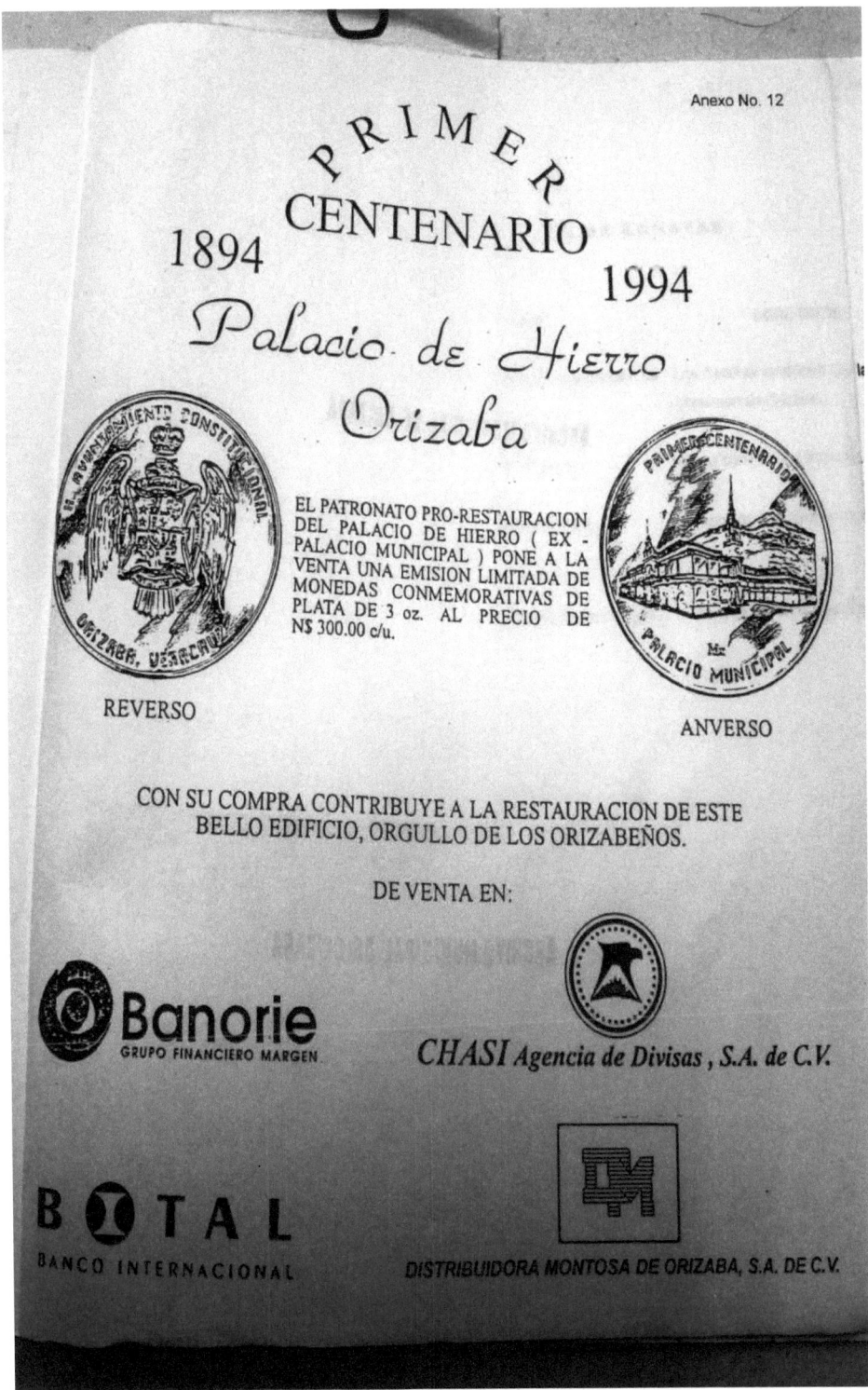

CELEBRATING ITS FIRST 100 YEARS

PRIMER CENTENARIO
1894 — 1994
Palacio de Hierro Orizaba

Anexo No. 12

EL PATRONATO PRO-RESTAURACION DEL PALACIO DE HIERRO (EX - PALACIO MUNICIPAL) PONE A LA VENTA UNA EMISION LIMITADA DE MONEDAS CONMEMORATIVAS DE PLATA DE 3 oz. AL PRECIO DE N$ 300.00 c/u.

REVERSO   ANVERSO

CON SU COMPRA CONTRIBUYE A LA RESTAURACION DE ESTE BELLO EDIFICIO, ORGULLO DE LOS ORIZABEÑOS.

DE VENTA EN:

CHASI Agencia de Divisas, S.A. de C.V.

DISTRIBUIDORA MONTOSA DE ORIZABA, S.A. DE C.V.

CELEBRATING ITS FIRST 100 YEARS

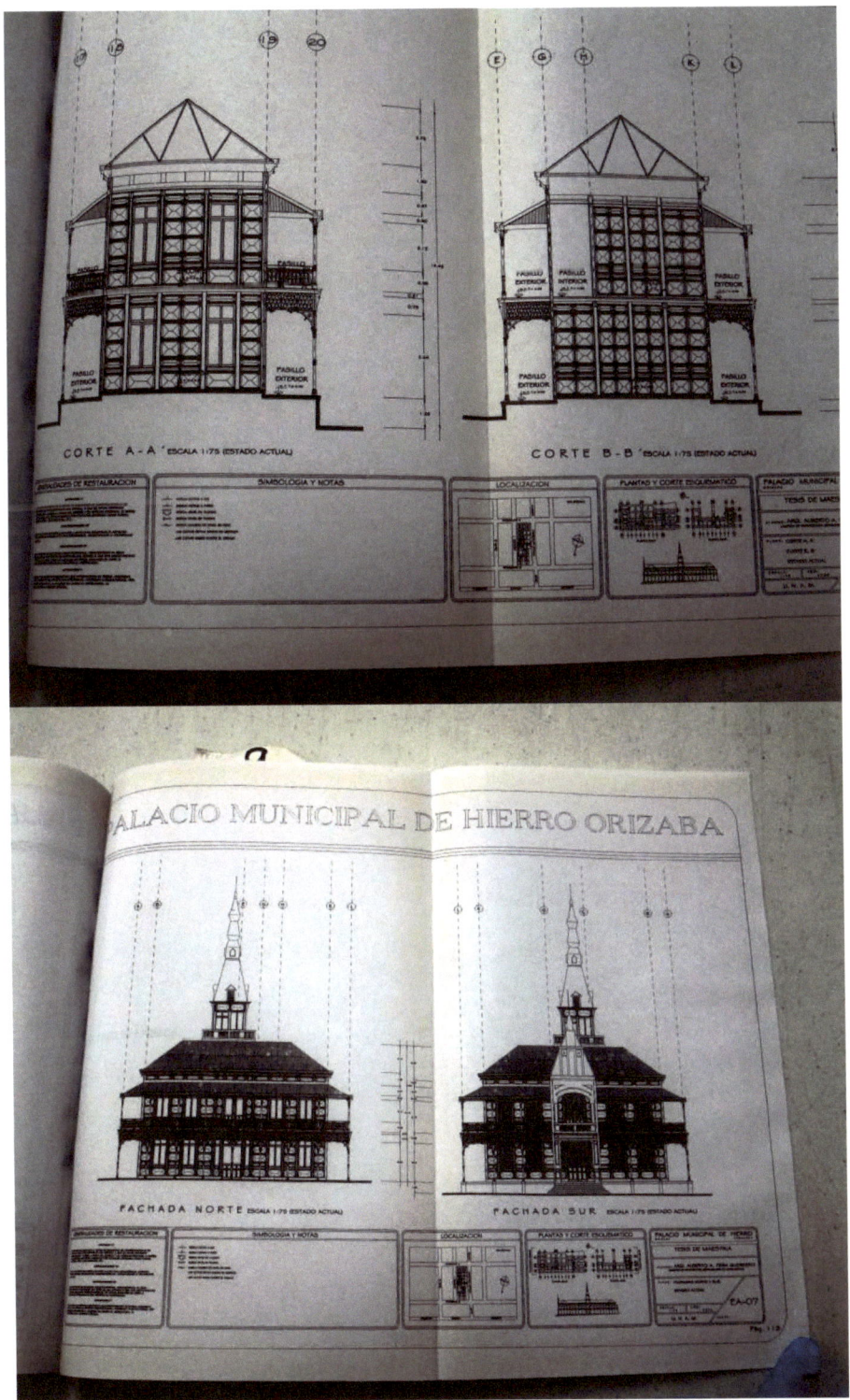

THE EIFFEL EXPLORATION SERIES   Constantine Issighos

PANORAMIC VIEW

Palacio de Hierro

Palacio de Hierro

THE EIFFEL EXPLORATION SERIES   Constantine Issighos

Palacio de Hierro

Palacio de Hierro

THE EIFFEL EXPLORATION SERIES　　　　　　　　　　　　　Constantine Issighos

Palacio de Hierro

CHURCH OF SANTA BARBARA

CHURCH OF SANTA BARBARA

Santa Rosalia is a port city located in the northern part of the Mexican State of Baja California. A regular ferry route connects it with the city of Guayamas, State of Sinaloa, on the opposite site of the Gulf of Mexico. The town of Santa Rosalia exhibits architecture of French influence and the cultural lifestyle and glamour of a bygone era.

Few towns have known the abrupt demographic highs and lows as Santa Rosalia. Life in this town was far from agreeable and sporadic civil interruptions were a common occurrence between the indigenous population and the controlling political powers of the city. If in some ways there were cordial relations between the European settlers and the town's mining company, there was a good deal of tension between the indigenous miners and the mine directors. In the 1880s, the culture of this town was full of paradoxes--it had Father Juan Rossi, an Italian priest who had just emigrated from the West Indies and it had a church designed by the French and built by the Belgians. It was a remote Mexican mining town, run by a French company, owned by the House of Rothschild of France.

The legend of Santa Rosalia's Church of Santa Barbara begins in 1868, when the very rich coppermine owners of the Boleo Mining Company, a subsidiary of the House of Rothschild, began constructing a network of roads and waterlines to supply the needs of the mine and miners. Ranches and farms developed next in order to complete the living necessities of the people in the area. One necessity, however, was overlooked-- a church for the citizens of the new town.

About that time, Alexandre Gustave Eiffel was designing and building pre-fabricated metal structures "on spec" in the hope that such structures would one day meet the needs of missionary churches in France's tropical colonies. The future Church of Santa Barbara was originally constructed as a prototype for a missionary church. Built in 1889 as part of the Paris Universal Exposition displays, it was supposed to demonstrate to interested   buyers that this metal structure was strong enough to withstand severe tropical weather. An additional element was that it was constructed with galvanized metal pieces to prevent weather corrosion. Its design of interlocked metal pieces became so popular that it won a first prize.

At the end of the Paris Universal Exposition, this structure was dismantled and placed in either a warehouse in Brussels, Belgium or somewhere in Baja California; it is not clear where. It remained there for nearly eight years when an official from the Boleo Mining Co. learned of its whereabouts, purchased it and shipped it to Santa Rosalia where the structure was re-assembled in 1898 to serve as a church. The happy residents of Santa Rosalia named it the Inglesia de Santa Barbara.

Another legend of the Santa Barbara Church is that in about 1896, a group of prominent town ladies asked Mrs. LaForgue, wife of the Director of the mine, to intercede with her husband to build a Catholic Church. Mr LaForgue agreed, but as he was on his way to Europe, the matter was postponed. A year later, while he was visiting Brussels, he came across a metallic church designed by Gustave Eiffel that was destined for Africa. Whoever had ordered this metallic church did so because wood was devoured by the African continent's white ants. It is still unknown why this church did not reach its original destination. When LaForgue saw it, he bought it and shipped it to Santa Rosalia.

The first recorded baptism in the newly erected church was performed by Father Juan Rossi, an Italian priest from the West Indies, on January 2, 1898. People in the region were cordial, so Santa Rosalia became a dynamic and versatile city. The inhabitants loved music, formed their own orchestras, invited sailors to their picnics, welcomed ships and saw them off. To be a resident of Santa Rosalia was something else. They had theatres where they showed French movies, and organized celebrations each year for New Year's, Carnival and Bastille Day. Today's overall town architecture is distinctly French. The town's main tourist attraction is still the Church of Santa Barbara.

Arriving in Santa Rosalia to view the church of Santa Barbara was full of travel challenges. The ferry which travels between Guaymas (mainland) and Santa Rosalia (Baja California) had delays and after 12 hours of waiting, I was told that it had not enough cargo to justify the 10 hours trip across the channel... Fortunately, I found someone who directed me to a Guaymas

office of the ASG Airoservice. The general manager, Ramon Enrique Ulba Lugo was very helpful especially when he found out that I was visiting Santa Rosalia to authenticate the origins of the church of Santa Barbara.
Weather conditions further delayed my crossing to Baja California. After 3 days of waiting, I finally crossed the channel aboard the 12 seat ASG Airoservice plane. The 30 minutes fly time was smooth and the panoramic view of the coast lines and channel was awesome.

To my pleasant surprise, I met Daniel upon arrival. For the duration of my 4 days in Santa Rosalia, Daniel became my personal guide and driver (at no charge) with instructions from Ramon to make my visiting time as productive as possible. Daniel assisted me with pictures, locations and introduced me to knowledgeable people of local history. My warmest appreciation to both.

Santa Barbara

SANTA ROSALIA WITH ITS OLD LOCOMOTIVE

METALIC INTERIOR ORNAMENTAL DECOR

THE EIFFEL EXPLORATION SERIES   Constantine Issighos

Santa Barbara

THE EIFFEL EXPLORATION SERIES   Constantine Issighos

Santa Barbara

Santa Barbara

THE EIFFEL EXPLORATION SERIES   Constantine Issighos

Santa Barbara

THE EIFFEL EXPLORATION SERIES
Constantine Issighos

Santa Barbara

Santa Barbara

INTERIOR STRUCTURAL SUPPORT COLUMN

THE EIFFEL EXPLORATION SERIES
Constantine Issighos

AN IMPESSIVE INTERIOS CURVULAR SPACE

Santa Barbara

EARLY 20th CENTURY PHOTO OF SANTA BARBARA CHURCH

SANTA BARBARA CHURCH IS THE FOCAL POINT OF MOST OF THE TOWN'S CULTURAL ACTIVITIES

THE EIFFEL EXPLORATION SERIES   Constantine Issighos

IGLESIA SANTA BARBARA
DE SANTA ROSALIA
DISEÑADA EN 1884
POR GUSTAVE EIFFEL
CONSTRUIDA EN 1887
EXPUESTA EN PARIS EN 1889
JUNTO CON LA TORRE EIFFEL,
ESTUVO EN BRUSELAS BELGICA
DESARMADA Y SE TRASLADO
A SANTA ROSALIA
INSTALANDOSE DE 1895 A 1897
DIC. 1997

A "MECCANO" STYLE METAL CHURCH WITH ITS THIN WALLS

.....SURROUNDED WITH A NEWER LANDSCAPE

INTERIOR AND EXTERIOR OD STAINED GLASS WINDOWS

SIMPLE ROOFING IRON STRUCTURE

THE EIFFEL EXPLORATION SERIES — Constantine Issighos

**A N IMPESSIVE STAINED GLASS WINDOW
WITH GEOMETRICAL DESIGN**

Santa Barbara

ROOF SUPPORT STRUCTURE

SIMPLE PROVINCIAL STYLE OF DOOR WAYS

THE EIFFEL EXPLORATION SERIES　　　　　　　　　　　Constantine Issighos

AN INDUNSTRIAL STYLE OF IRON ARTWORKS

Santa Barbara

WOODEN SIDE DOOR

Santa Barbara

THE EIFFEL EXPLORATION SERIES — Constantine Issighos

Santa Barbara

Santa Barbara

THE EIFFEL EXPLORATION SERIES Constantine Issighos

Santa Barbara

THE EIFFEL EXPLORATION SERIES — Constantine Issighos

Santa Barbara

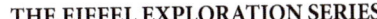

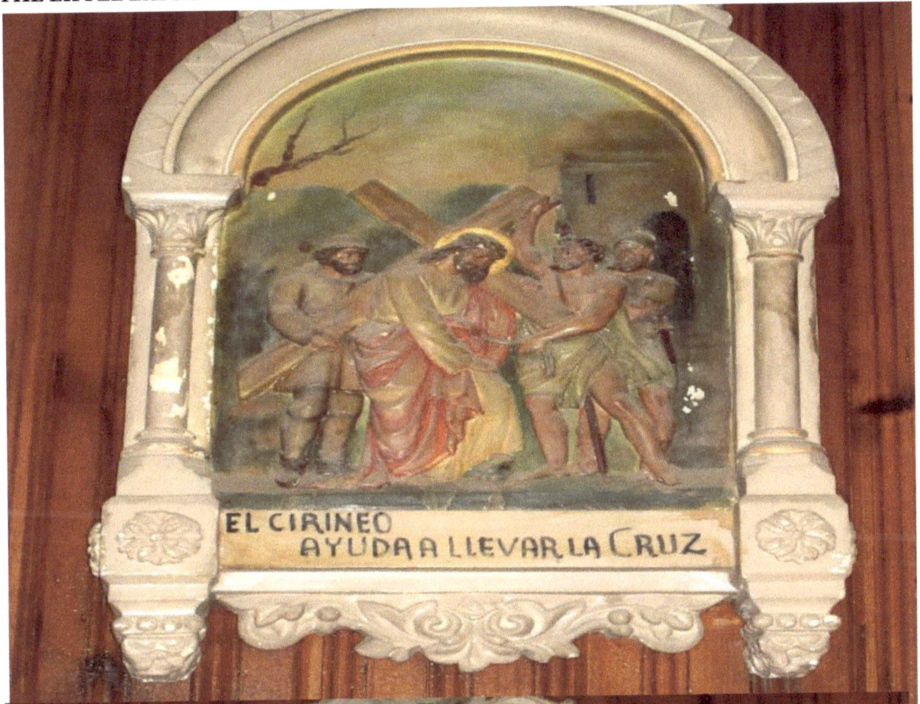
EL CIRINEO
AYUDA A LLEVAR LA CRUZ

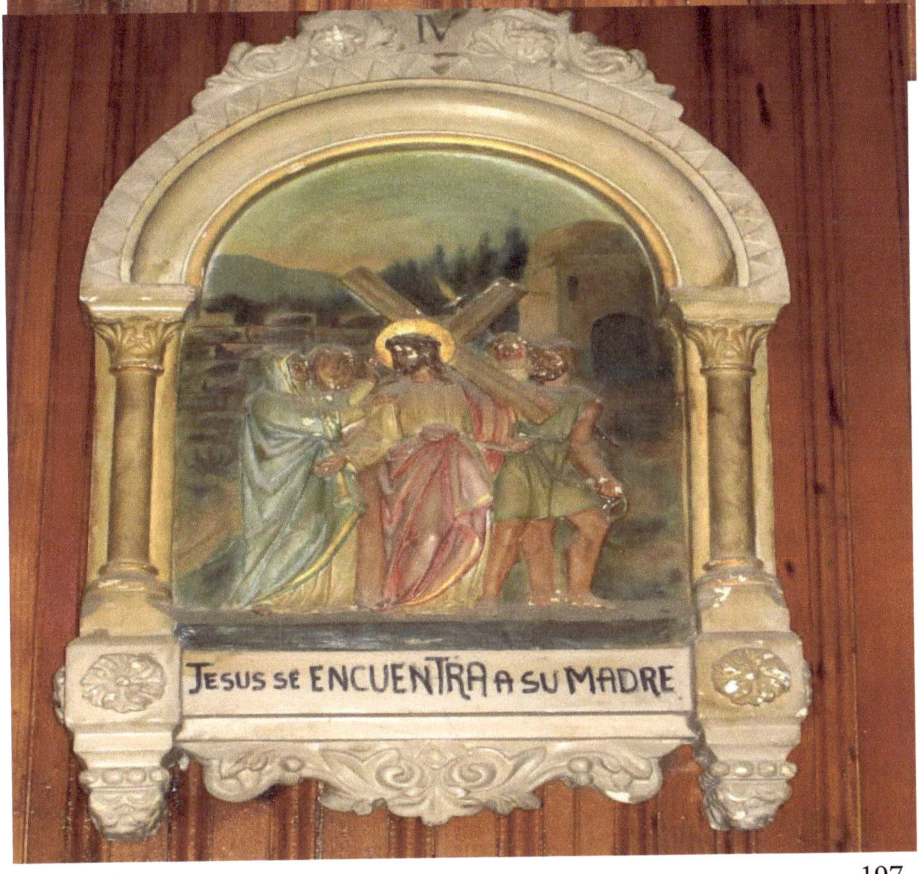
IV
JESUS SE ENCUENTRA A SU MADRE

Ecuador

PALACIO CRYSTAL

CRYSTAL PALACE OF GUAYAQUIL

The Crystal Palace is located in Guayaquil, in south of Ecuador. The city is the largest and most populous one with about 2.2 million people in the metropolitan area. It is also the nation's main port. Guayaquil was founded on July 15, 1438 by the Spanish Conquistador Francisco de Orellana. By this declaration, the already existing village became the future capital of Ecuador.

Due to its Spanish commercial wealth, Guayaquil was repeatedly attacked and looted by English and French pirates. In 1687, more than 250 French pirates, under the command of Captain Groniet, attacked and looted Guayaquil, killing more than one hundred and taking village women as concubines.

The historical development of the city of Guayaquil led to the building of many notable structures, such as the Palacio Principal, the Mercado Artesanal and the present day Crystal Palace. The Crystal Palace is a cast-iron and plate-glass building. At the time of its reconstruction, it had the largest window glass ever seen in a building in Ecuador. With its clear walls, it does not require interior lights during the day.

Lured by its striking architecture, people have chosen the Crystal Palace as the venue for major cultural expositions and important national and local, as well as public and private, celebrations. It is considered one of the city's most emblematic buildings and one of the most important cultural centers of Ecuador. The building's original name was The Old South Malecon Market where for nearly eight decades from its inauguration in 1905, it served as a fruit, vegetable and dairy produce market. The Mercado Sur (as it was known) was surrounded by support bars which were replaced by glass plates. Today, thanks to the urban regeneration of the Main Port, the building has been transformed into an architectural jewel which is the pride of the city.

The original engineering design was done by Gustave Eiffel. The actual construction of the building began in 1904 by the Vesuelan architect Francisco Manrique Paganis, who was a direct representative of Gustave

Eiffel. Its structural and ornamental parts were forged in Eiffel's associate workshop Varhaus Co. de Jegar Ingenieurs – Constructiurs of Brussels, Belgium. The parts were shipped to its present location in 1906. The building has been through a number of major and minor remodelling processes to meet local standards and serve its present purpose.

    The Crystal Palace is fully transparent due to its iron and glass walls. It is made of wrought iron and its hierarchical design reflected Eiffel's practical brilliance as a designer. It offered practical advantages that no conventional building could match and, above all, embodied the Eiffel spirit of metallic engineering innovation.

    The current geometry of the Crystal Palace is a classical example of the balance of form, structure and aesthetics. The shape and size of the whole building is based around the size of its plate-glass windows and the entire structure is scaled to their dimensions. This means that the whole perimeter surface of the identical plate-glass panels forms a huge open-space gallery.

    Even though Eiffel was able to draw on his considerable engineering experience for the original structural design of The Old South Malecon Market, the scale of his achievement is extraordinary by the standards of his time. In his design, he displayed efficiencies, energy-saving techniques and innovation. What is doubly remarkable is the fact that he exhibited solid confidence in the novice skills of the Venezuelan born and French trained civil engineer Francisco Manrique Paganis 1875 – 1940 to complete the job.

    One must remember that Eiffel was a structural engineer who designed, or forged--in his various workshops--works of practical nature. With the exception of the Paris Tower and the Statute of Liberty, Eiffel did not designed or build monuments per se. He was an innovator of unique designs that were mostly casual works and part of his daily routine. Eiffel's direct involvement in the actual construction of the Tower and the Statute of Liberty are his only recorded physical participation in any given project.

    Written contracts were rarely signed between Eiffel and his close associates. Such legalistic practices were followed (sometimes) for major engineering works. Most "proofs" of Eiffel's involvement in a given metal or iron projects are secondary in nature and are supported by various factual occurrences. This is also the case with the current Crystal Palace.

Crystal Palace

THE EIFFEL EXPLORATION SERIES — Constantine Issighos

Crystal Palace

Crystal Palace

THE EIFFEL EXPLORATION SERIES — Constantine Issighos

A MAGNIFICENT ORNAMENTAL IRON STRUCTURE

Crystal Palace

Crystal Palace

THE EIFFEL EXPLORATION SERIES   Constantine Issighos

Crystal Palace

Crystal Palace

THE EIFFEL EXPLORATION SERIES　　　　　　　　　　Constantine Issighos

Crystal Palace

THE EIFFEL EXPLORATION SERIES
Constantine Issighos

Crystal Palace

THE EIFFEL EXPLORATION SERIES — Constantine Issighos

Crystal Palace

THE EIFFEL EXPLORATION SERIES — Constantine Issighos

Crystal Palace

Crystal Palace

THE EIFFEL EXPLORATION SERIES   Constantine Issighos

Crystal Palace

THE EIFFEL EXPLORATION SERIES   Constantine Issighos

Crystal Palace

The original *The Old South Malecon Market* without the glass walls

Index

France	7
US	35
Mexico	87
Ecuador	199
Index	226